To Sheila

Sonny – 'For the Good Times'

SONNY
For the Good Times

HILLGATE PUBLISHING LTD.

Sonny Knowles – in conversation with Frank Corr

AN EMERALD CLASSIC PUBLICATION

First published in 2009
by Hillgate Publishing Ltd.
The Village Pump, Batterstown,
Co. Meath, Ireland
Phone No.: 01-8241005
Email: hillgate1@eircom.net
Web: www.hillgatepublishing.ie

ISBN: 978-0-9541819-2-5

Cover design by Dermot O'Connor & Associates Ltd.
Typeset by Computertype, Dublin
Printed in Ireland by W. & G. Baird Ltd., Dublin

Contents

	Preface by Ronan Collins	7
	Introduction by Frank Corr	11
Chapter 1	Liberties Boy	27
Chapter 2	Drimnagh Days	33
	Tribute from Joe Duffy	38
Chapter 3	Making Suits and Music	41
Chapter 4	Sheila	49
	Tribute from Paddy Cole	59
Chapter 5	Swinging and Singing	61
	Tribute from Earl Gill	70
Chapter 6	Showband Days – and Nights	73
Chapter 7	Come to the Cabaret	93
	Tribute from Tony Kenny	108
Chapter 8	Checkpoint Charlie	111
	Tribute from Paul O'Reilly	122
Chapter 9	All that Jazz	125
	Tribute from Pat Egan	135
Chapter 10	Radio Days	137
	Tribute from Jim Farley	148
Chapter 11	Cancer	151
	To a Happy End – Professor John Reynolds	164
	Tribute from Sil Fox	167
Chapter 12	Comeback	169

Acknowledgements

Many people contributed to this book and I thank each and every one who played a part in the enterprise. The original idea came from publisher Des O'Neill of Hillgate Limited who inspired the project from the beginning, with Joan O'Sullivan always there with support and administrative expertise. Frank Dunne and the Dunne Family supported the book from the outset while Pat Egan, Paul O'Reilly, Ronan Collins, Jim Farley, Earl Gill, Joe Duffy, Paddy Cole, Jim Bartley and many others from the entertainment industry made valuable contributions. Geraldine gathered family pictures in Australia, Andrea Smith played a key role in research and publicity, Jean Gibbons and Billy Porter meticulously edited the text, Pat Beausang created the design and typography and we were in the safe hands of Bairds, our printer. Lorraine O'Sullivan was our photographer, thanks to Mark Condron, *Sunday Tribune* for the photo of Sonny and Tony Kenny and my thanks also go to those who contributed pictures or allowed their work to be published in the book. We made valiant attempts to contact all the photographers involved but if we missed anybody, please accept our thanks and apologies.

My wife Irene lived with the book as it evolved and allowed me the time and space for writing.

But the real creators of this book are Sonny and Sheila Knowles, in whose lovely, welcoming home, I spent pleasant hours drinking coffee, scoffing Custard Creams and listening as they told their story.

It was a labour of love.

– F C

'Me and Dad' ...
Ronan Collins

'**D**ad' is a term of familiarity used between jazz musicians when they chat together and I am honoured that I am often called by that name by Sonny Knowles.

I have been an admirer of Sonny since the mid Sixties, when he was the big cabaret star in Dublin and I was playing drums in a pub band. To me, he was the consummate professional and remains so today.

Sonny is first and foremost a musician, who learned his trade playing the saxophone in the Dublin dance orchestras of the 1950s and later developing his unique singing talent with the Pacific Showband and then as a cabaret artiste. Throughout that highly successful career, he has never thought about himself as a 'star'. His approach has always been based on the basic attributes of a true professional – turn up punctually, sober and well dressed, perform, get paid and go home. That is not to say that he does not enjoy the social side of the business – indeed I have never met a more decent, kind and friendly person than Sonny Knowles.

We got to know each other shortly after I began presenting programmes on RTÉ in 1979. I discovered some of the LPs he had made and began to play them on air. In particular I liked the albums he had recorded for Rex Records on which he sang popular songs arranged by Jim Doherty, Johnny Tate and Noel Kelehan. These tracks have retained their freshness and appeal up to the present day.

Sonny approaches every song he sings with meticulous care and style, which has won him the admiration of seasoned professional musicians everywhere he performs. That approach is the same whether he is in the recording studio, on the stage of the National Concert Hall or in a small Dublin pub or whether he is accompanied by session musicians, the National Concert Orchestra or a lad playing the spoons. Over the years, he has developed a trademark series of hand signals to his backing musicians indicating when he wants the key changed up or down. They always work because Sonny only sings songs that they all know.

We have met at the many charity events which Sonny supports and also often in RTÉ where he has been a frequent presenter, performer and guest over the years. This is no accident because any radio or TV presenter knows that featuring Sonny Knowles on the show guarantees a significant increase in the viewing or listening figures. In two words – Sonny delivers.

There is also an element of steel in this nice and decent man, which enables him to know when somebody might be trying to 'pull a fast one'. This same strength has helped him battle successfully with two episodes of cancer. In those dark days he fought bravely, supported as always by the other part of a great double act – his wife Sheila.

When Sonny was battling his way back from illness, our radio show phone lines were always busy with people from all over the country enquiring about his progress and wishing him well. I was delighted to be able to keep in touch and to pass on the news to the listeners. Some 18 months after his second operation, I was able to announce that Sonny had indeed recovered and was preparing for a comeback. I was delighted to be able to play a role in that remarkable return to the entertainment scene. Paul O'Reilly invited me to select some tracks from Sonny's LPs, which he planned to include on a new CD to be called *The Very Best of Sonny Knowles*. Sonny himself was somewhat dubious about the project as he felt that a CD would not sell at this stage of his career. In fact it went Platinum, selling more than 15,000 copies – and nobody was more surprised than Sonny. I also played a cameo role in his comeback concert, organising a band of musicians who knew Sonny well and sitting in myself on drums. The comeback concert at the National Concert Hall was a triumph for Sonny, who was understandably very nervous before going on stage. He need not have worried.

Once he walked out before the audience, you could feel the warmth and love wafting up from the auditorium, and from the first bars of the first song, Sonny was back where he loved to be – entertaining an audience.

Sonny Knowles is a charismatic entertainer, an accomplished musician, a lovely decent man and a good friend, by whom I am honoured to be called 'Dad'.

Full Circle

Frank Corr recalls six decades of music that have marked the career of Sonny Knowles.

Good music lasts.

Just a few hours ago I was on the seafront in Bray as a few thousand people sang along with a Beatles tribute band. They were of all ages – young kids, teenagers, married couples, parents and granddads like myself. The music was infectious, witty, smart and as fresh as when we all sang *Yeah, Yeah, Yeah* in the Swinging Sixties.

Sonny Knowles, the subject of this book, also sings songs that last. Indeed, he has been singing them now for close on 50 years and, with his inimitable tone, sense of timing and phrasing and warm personality, they too are as fresh as newly laid eggs.

His early musical influences were also mine. At the Knowles home in Chancery Lane in the Dublin Liberties and at the Corr home in the *Angela's Ashes* area of Limerick, radios stayed tuned in the mornings to the BBC Light Programme, from which the strict-tempo dance music of Victor Sylvester soothed the furrowed brows of harassed mothers whose dreams had yet to extend to the cutting-edge technologies of washing machines and refrigerators.

While my mother did her morning chores to the rhythms of the foxtrot and quickstep, my father would turn the dial until he found Glen Miller, Tommy Dorsey or maybe Bing Crosby. 'That', he would tell me, 'is jazz.'

To a little Limerick boy in the 1940s, jazz was already exciting and smacked of danger. Even then I had heard of gangsters. It was different from my earliest musical experiences, which were the Savoy operas of Gilbert and Sullivan, much loved by my grandmother who would bang out the tunes on our piano and when the opportunity arose would march me off to a local production of *The Mikado* or *The Gondoliers*. So while other kids were stood up at parties to sing their nursery rhymes, I performed *Tit Willow*.

Songs were sung in the Knowles and Corr homes – both to accompany work and, more formally, at an evening tea party. With my mother on our vintage Collard and Collard upright and various uncles and aunts singing pieces from opera or Victorian ballads, competition for a spot was as keen as anything on *The X Factor*.

The first pop song I remember was *Put Another Nickel in the Nickelodeon*, which was sung by all the kids at the Model Primary School because it had been 'condemned' by a local priest who took exception to the line *All I Want is Loving You and Music, Music, Music*, which he said represented a shallow and materialistic view of life. But that did not prevent my mother playing it on the piano with the window open, right across the street from the Redemptorist Monastery. Her own favourite from those days was *Red Roses for a Blue Lady* by Donald Peers – a song I considered to be altogether too mushy.

Sonny recalls playing with the Post Office band on bandstands in Bray and around Dublin, and it was another such bandstand in the People's Park in Limerick that helped me expand my love for music. On Sundays the local Boherbuoy Brass and Reed Band would give a recital and it was there that I first heard versions of pieces like the *Poet and Peasant* and *William Tell* overtures, which have remained favourites of mine to this day. The band would also play the marches of John Philip Sousa who once conducted an orchestra in Limerick in which my grandmother played the violin. Some years later when I was a teenager, I stopped off to listen to the Boherbuoy and a little lad stood there, waving his arms, 'conducting' the music. It was a very young Bill Whelan, who grew up to be one of the finest musicians which this country has produced.

Just as I remember where I was when John F. Kennedy was shot (at the cinema), so do I clearly remember the first time I heard rock'n'roll. I was in bed with measles or mumps or some such childhood malady and my mother turned on the radio to keep me company. It was 1.15pm and the Donnelly's sponsored programme was being broadcast. Then out of the radio came a sound and a beat that changed my whole feeling about music. I was 14 and had just heard Bill Haley and the Comets sing *Rock Around the Clock* for the first time. From that moment I was hooked on rock'n'roll.

Hot on the heels of Bill Haley came Fats Domino, Little Richard, Gene Vincent and, of course, Elvis. My grandmother, then in her late eighties, was also an Elvis fan and would tell me that he had 'a fine baritone voice'. The next few years were dominated by rock'n'roll, which was interrupted now and again by the need to do some study at St. Munchin's College. We all played in little bands (I was a rather inept drummer), ran 'hops' which proved to be a nice little earner, spent our meagre pocket money on records and knickerbocker glories, and lived the good life.

Then just after my seventeenth birthday, my father died. I completed my final year at school, did the Leaving Certificate, worked for a few months in a dead-end office job and then became a journalist.

Getting on the staff of the *Limerick Weekly Echo* opened many musical doors. I could walk into concerts and recitals free of charge, experience an esoteric new world of chamber and symphonic music, enjoy grand opera and, best of all, get a pass to the local ballrooms.

Within weeks in my new job, I had established myself as 'dance columnist' and so began a close involvement with the showbands. While still at school, I had sneaked off a few times to watch The Clipper Carlton at the Stella Ballroom, which had a large statue of the Blessed Virgin watching over the dancers and reminding them of their moral responsibilities. By far the biggest attraction there was Brendan Bowyer (who was in my class at infant school) when he appeared with The Royal Showband. Now however I was immersed in a 'shower of showbands' whose managers craved publicity, as did the local ballroom operators. It was around this time that I first heard the singing of Sonny Knowles when he toured with The Pacific. To be honest, Sean Fagan was the big attraction in the band but Sonny had his own following. The bands occasionally stayed over on a Saturday night and on the following morning, an eclectic group of local and visiting musicians would gather in Geary's Hotel for a big band jam session. Sonny says that he never sat in on these sessions as The Pacific always returned to Dublin after a gig.

Limerick had its own big band in those days, fronted by Bob Madden, and it was from this group that six guys formed The Monarchs Showband, which had Tommy Drennan as lead singer and included in its lineup Jim Connolly who was to make a very successful career as a sculptor and potter. He also pioneered the movement, which saw hundreds of Dublin families move to the West of Ireland and a less stressful lifestyle. All were good friends of mine, particularly the manager Ray Heraty, and it was not long before I was recruited as the band's publicist. The Monarchs' first single was *Boolavogue*, which was a big hit and they had a Christmas No. 1 with Tommy singing *O Holy Night*. This was a peculiar record as the first part was a remastered recording of an old tape on which Tommy had sung with the Redemptorist Church Choir as a boy soprano. This was followed by a few instrumental bars, after which Tommy changed to his own distinctive voice which had seemingly 'broken' miraculously in the interim. I was fortunate enough to play a cameo role in this recording as I was also in the choir when that early tape was made and so I can claim to have been part of a Christmas No. 1 record. Watch out for that if you are ever in a Limerick pub quiz.

The Monarchs' most enterprising project however was *50 Years After*, an LP made in 1966 to commemorate the 50th Anniversary of the Easter Rising. The band was supplemented by a few session musicians including the great trumpet player Joe McIntyre, and the arrangements were mostly by Bryan Meehan. The songs were chosen by Nollaig Ó Gadhra, a long-time Irish language activist, who included numbers as diverse as *My Old Fenian Gun, The Dying Rebel* and *Sean South of Garryowen*. There was also some poetry and prose. We launched the LP at Jurys Hotel in Dame Street, Dublin and during the party I was taken aside by Charles Acton, the venerable music critic of *The Irish Times* and told that there was a distinct danger that everybody connected with the record could be charged with treason. The reason, he explained, was that we had recorded a vocal version of the National Anthem in an arrangement, which had not been approved by the Director of the Army School of Music. Fortunately that august personage either never came across the LP or tactfully chose to ignore our treasonable act.

The Monarchs were a creative lot. When dances were banned during Lent, they formed a Variety Group which toured the area rather than take the familiar path to England. The band was supplemented by Anne Mulqueen, a legendary traditional singer, Teresa Daly, a dancer and myself, who had the job of booking the halls, getting the posters displayed, taking the money at the door and acting as MC and link-man. The band members doubled as actors in a few dodgy sketches which we had cobbled together. We were on a circuit competing with amateur drama festivals and a travelling magician, and the reception would vary from the ecstatic to the decidedly hostile. On another occasion, the band decided to make a pilot radio programme, which it would try to sell to Radio Éireann whose musical output was almost entirely from Dublin. We hired a local theatre and set up a recording studio in a van outside the back door. Our guests were We 4, a folk group whose members included Suzanne Murphy, later to become an internationally renowned opera singer and the show was presented by Noel McCaul. Called *Pop Down South*, it was a slick and entertaining piece of live radio which never did get broadcast, but which reappeared on a CD which Ray Heraty produced in 2008. The Monarchs also realised that the showband era would not last forever and, in anticipation of its end, they set up a business called 'Monarch Enterprises', which was engaged in screen printing and graphic design. This particular enterprise however proved to be even more mercurial than the showbands.

Donie Collins was the leader of the other big Limerick showband. He was from the village of Askeaton and a great character. On one occasion his boys were setting up their gear in a country hall for a 9pm to 2am dance when the owner wanted to know why they were not playing. 'It's only ten to nine, Boss,' Donie said, 'We will be up and running at nine.'

The owner's reaction was to walk back down the large empty ballroom, turn around and declare: 'Well alright Mr. Collins – but it had better be good.'

Pat Hayes was the local ballroom king. His Oyster Ballroom at Dromkeen, a crossroads about 12 miles from Limerick City, was a mecca for dancers within a 60 mile radius and he attracted all the big names to what would now be seen as a glorified warehouse. It had little in the line of luxury or facilities for musicians but its location and Pat's enterprise made it a lucrative venue for bands. Pat was among the pioneers of the country dance hall and was always prepared to splash out on booking visiting stars. It was through him that I got to meet people like Jim Reeves, Hank Locklin, The Bachelors, The Shadows, Adam Faith, Sid Phillips, John Dankworth and Cleo Laine, all of whom appeared at the Oyster. When John Dankworth brought his Big Band there around 1966, his programme featured modern arrangements, many of which had complex time signatures. The men and women who had gathered at opposite sides of the ballroom, according to the etiquette of the day, waited patiently, in vain and in silence for a tune to which they could dance. Eventually a delegation of three lads in caps approached the bandleader, who evidently expected to be complimented on his music. Beckoning the great musician, their leader said: 'Sure we can't dance to that. Do you know *The Boys from the County Armagh*?'

Pat Hayes had worthy competition from Jack O'Rourke who had a big ballroom in Newcastlewest at the other end of the county and a Caherconlish committee who had built a hall with the novel idea of converting it into a church when the debt had been cleared. This little hall could attract most of the big bands as well as overseas artistes and it was the first Irish stop for The Clancy Brothers during their homecoming tour in the late Sixties. The whole scene changed however, with the arrival of the Reynolds ballrooms in Limerick. The Jetland was the newest, biggest and most luxurious of the chain and when it opened on a site in Caherdavin, it removed the need for Limerick city dancers to travel to Dromkeen or Newcastlewest. The manager was Maxie Muldoon, who had a long association with the Clipper Carlton and over the next decade or so he hosted all of the big showbands as well as acts like The Everly Brothers, Freddie and the Dreamers, The Searchers and Johnny Cash. Jetland was one of the last Reynolds ballrooms to open and it probably arrived just after the showband business had peaked. It tended to fill on Saturday nights but midweek gigs were often poorly attended. On one such evening, the late Nelius O'Connell remarked to me that: 'One day soon these places will be supermarkets.' He was correct for within a few years Jetland was actually converted into a Dunnes Stores.

The first sign that the showband era was beginning to fade was when small 'beat clubs' began to open, initially in Dublin, but later in other cities including Limerick. Danny Hughes brought the club scene to Limerick, operating from a converted garage in Post Office Lane. The clubs hosted up and coming rock groups and it was here that I first heard Thin Lizzy, Them and Granny's Intentions. This was new, brash, noisy, rhythmic music played by lads with very long hair, worn jeans and black t-shirts. It was largely incomprehensible to me but the kids loved it and we began to cover the beat scene extensively in the *Limerick Weekly Echo*. Granny's Intentions had local members from Limerick and they became a fairly large attraction in this country and in the UK. They played a set for me on one occasion when I organised a concert for a local festival – sandwiched on the bill between a school of Irish dancing and an operatic soprano.

Appearances by international stars were a rarity in Limerick until the late Sixties, although Eddie Calvert had brought his Golden Trumpet to the Stella Ballroom in 1958. Emile Ford was the first major Sixties act to play at the Stella. The gig was promoted by Peter Prendergast who managed The Dixies and also ran the Arcadia Ballroom in Cork. Emile played to a packed house and was quickly followed by a succession of visiting acts including Brian Poole and the Tremeloes, Acker Bilk, Kenny Ball and the great Roy Orbison, who played two sell-out concerts at the 1,500 seater Savoy Theatre. Interestingly many of these acts would not attract full houses, partly because they tended to play midweek dates and partly because the scene was already moving away from the ballrooms to clubs and bars.

Ronnie Drew and the Dubliners were the first big 'cabaret act' in Limerick, although their gigs were referred to as 'ballad sessions'. It was 'standing room only' when they played at the Royal George, a venue which also hosted The Wolfe Tones, The Johnsons, The Pattersons, Pecker Dunne and The Ludlow Trio. Then, just as I was leaving Limerick to live in Dublin, a huge new attraction began to play pub venues in Limerick and Clare. His name was Christy Moore.

Christy was also the star of the first really big outdoor music festival to take place in Ireland. It was held annually in a field in Lisdoonvarna, Co. Clare and was immortalised in Christy's famous song. It was here that I first heard Jackson Browne, Bananarama, Moving Hearts and an amazing a cappella group called The Flying Pickets who held an enormous and boisterous crowd spellbound for almost an hour, using only their voices. Lisdoonvarna was a place of annual pilgrimage but my last visit was a sad occasion when a number of young people were drowned while swimming off a nearby beach.

The club scene was booming when I came to work in Dublin in 1969. Love stories were beginning every night at Zhivago, where I first heard bands like Chips and Stepaside. Sonny Knowles was then King of Cabaret in Dublin, hosting all the big acts of the day at the Drake Inn in Finglas and the Tudor Room. My favourite cabaret spot was the Braemor Rooms, especially when the star was Josef Locke who would have the crowd on its feet with his lusty renditions of *The Soldier's Dream* and *Goodbye*. The dinner show at the Braemor offered an exceptional combination of good food and good music presided over by Eamon Geraghty and Muriel Quinn. Another great package was the Saturday evening dinner dance at the Green Isle Hotel on the Naas Road, where Sonny was often the featured artiste. At one such dinner dance, organised by members of the confectionery trade, we won a very large plastic bag of assorted candy, which our children were certain to enjoy. Driving home there seemed to be Gardaí everywhere and we were duly pulled over and asked to open the boot of the car. The Gardaí took a very keen interest in our spot prize, opening the bag with close attention and great care. It transpired that earlier in the evening the Sallins Train Robbery had taken place and the Gardaí thought they might just have stumbled on some of the booty. All they got, however, were a few Mars bars and lollipops.

My first contact with Pat Quinn was when he opened a Quinnsworth supermarket in Phibsboro and I was covering the event for *Business and Finance* magazine. He called a selection of journalists up from the crowd and asked us to name our favourite charity. He then wrote a cheque for £100 for each nominated charity and handed them out to us. He was a warm and generous man with a great sense of fun and we met regularly as he expanded his supermarket chain. After he had sold out to Galen Weston, Pat bought the Country Club at Kilternan from the Oppermann family and converted it into the Pat Quinn Club. This was to be the most innovative entertainment venue ever developed in Ireland. There was a golf course, a ski slope, a children's play area, a hotel, a restaurant and a cabaret room, which would host all the big stars of the day. It opened, I think, with The Bachelors and went on to attract an array of UK cabaret artistes. But it was also hit by the infamous oil crisis of 1973, which brought soaring energy prices, fuel shortages, long queues at petrol stations and even electricity outages. It became impossible for most people to get to Kilternan and despite Pat's great effort, the club closed.

The closing of another iconic Dublin venue, the Theatre Royal, deprived the city of a somewhere large enough to host top international acts. The Beatles and The Beach Boys had appeared at the Adelphi Cinema in Middle Abbey Street, which had minimal stage facilities, while Ella Fitzgerald, Oscar Peterson and even Duke Ellington and His Orchestra had played in the Metropole Cinema on O'Connell Street. Some years later a promoter got the idea of putting Chris de Burgh into the Main Hall of the RDS and while the venue was far from comfortable, it could hold around 4,000 people. The gigs were a sell-out and led to the RDS hosting many other international acts including Abba, James Last, Paul Simon and many more. Paul Simon and Art Garfunkel were later to bring their *Concert in Central Park* to the jumping arena of the RDS, a venue still popular with many of the big world acts like Bruce Springsteen and the E Street Band. The first big concert there however featured The Stylistics, one of whom was reported as being amazed at the 'Irish Ditch', a large mound used in show jumping events. 'Who's buried there, Man?' he asked a toffy RDS official.

It was probably U2, however, who made outdoor concerts really popular. They appeared at race courses and other large venues as soon as they became famous, and the idea of paying big bucks to stand in the rain became very popular with a younger generation. The first really memorable outdoor concert I attended was The Rolling Stones at Slane in 1982. I brought along my two young children and a warning from their mother that I should be on the lookout for drug taking or thuggery. We brought along a picnic, which we spread out on the grassy slope (yes – you could do that then), and I kept an ear out for any suspicious conversations. Behind me was a group of young women whose main topic of chat was who they had managed

SONNY – *FOR THE GOOD TIMES*

to get as babysitters for the day. Even in 1982, The Stones and Sonny Knowles were sharing fans.

Slane was a huge annual attraction in the Eighties and enabled me to catch acts like Queen, David Bowie and Bob Dylan. By far the most exciting concert was the visit of Bruce Springsteen in 1985. With nine-year-old son Damian in tow, we arrived at Slane precisely at 3pm and, as we were walking through the gates, the sound of *Born in the USA* was already pounding through the trees. Yes – the Boss was on stage, on time and was about to deliver a three hour gig. It was by far the best concert I had ever attended in my life up to that point and has only been matched by subsequent visits of Bruce to the Point and the RDS.

On another level, it was always a wonderful musical experience to dip into the Dublin jazz scene. One of my favourite spots was the South County Hotel in Stillorgan (now the Stillorgan Park), where Jim Doherty would assemble a big band of Dublin's most professional musicians, including one Sonny Knowles on baritone sax, sitting alongside his sidekick Jim Farley on tenor. It was at one of these gigs that I first heard Honor Heffernan sing and was thrilled by the unique quality of her voice, her natural jazz phrasing and her ability to communicate with her audience. She is one of the most talented Irish female jazz singers of her generation and continues to pack out the John Field Room at the National Concert Hall with the Jim Doherty Trio in their regular *We're Old Fashioned* series of concerts.

Honor sang many times for the National Jazz Society, which I joined in the mid Eighties, often with the great Louis Stewart on guitar. The NJS was headed by Alan Smith and it promoted a series of jazz gigs featuring the best of available talent from the UK, the USA and Europe. I became secretary for a few years and, accompanied by fellow committee member Billy Porter (of Guinness fame), I had the pleasant task of meeting musicians like Ruby Braff, Scott Hamilton, Ralph Sutton, Warren Vaché, Ken Peplowski, Axel Zwingenberger, Peter Appleyard and Kenny Davern, often greeting them at the airport and conveying them to their respective gigs. My favourite visiting jazzman was Spike Robinson, a gentle American who played his sax in much the same way that Sonny Knowles sings songs – with perfect pitch, a warm tone, immaculate phrasing and an appreciation of the primacy of melody.

The most ambitious enterprise undertaken by the NJS was a performance of Louis Stewart's jazz suite *Joycenotes* shortly before it was recorded in Norway in 1992. The piece had been commissioned by the Arts Council in 1981 and was premiered at the Guinness Cork Jazz Festival the following year. It comprises selected readings from *Ulysses* and jazz interpretations of these passages. Louis put a band of his close collaborators together for the Dublin performance, which was staged in the Royal Marine Hotel, Dun Laoghaire, but unfortunately they played to a rather small audience. My abiding memory therefore is not the wonderful readings and music, but of wondering how on Earth we would manage to pay the bills. The National Jazz Society later morphed into the Dublin Jazz Society and some members were also involved in the Improvised Music Company which has brought outstanding jazz to Dublin over the years.

Jazz was a regular topic over the months I spent talking to Sonny and Sheila Knowles as this book began to take shape. In particular, we spoke about the Cork Jazz Festival which enabled Irish audiences to hear almost all of the great names in world jazz. When the festival was sponsored by John Player, I had the great privilege of meeting and talking with Ella Fitzgerald, George Shearing, Oscar Peterson, and Cleo Laine. When Guinness took over the festival, not just as sponsor but as organiser, I got to play a cameo role in the press office and, in the process, met with an array of jazz legends. Over a period of 25 years, I was able to listen to every genre of jazz and to experience playing and singing that enormously widened my appreciation of this most creative of musical forms.

Meanwhile, of course, Sonny Knowles continued to reign as King of Cabaret in Dublin – although he did not have it all his own way. For many years, Tony Kenny played to full houses in Jurys Cabaret (with Jim Doherty as musical director) and, outside the capital, the one and only Joe Dolan was something of a national institution. As Sonny remarked to me, 'If you put him on in a field in the middle of a bog, he would fill it.'

Somewhere along the line, probably in the early Nineties, I left popular music – or rather it left me. Suddenly I found myself going to gigs featuring Full Circle (a reincarnation of the great Greenbeats), or enjoying artistes who had made their name a decade or two earlier and were still touring their greatest hits. Thanks to my children and 'Fab Vinny', I watched the early years of MTV and tried to keep up with the garage bands whose demo tracks were played by Dave Fanning on the radio, but when the children reached adulthood, I had no real means, nor reason, to stay in touch.

It was a pleasant surprise, therefore, to look in on Glastonbury this year and to discover that with bands like Kings of Leon, Glasvegas and Blur, good tunes and tight harmonies have not entirely gone away. What jumped out at me from the Festival lineup however was that the headliners had all been around for a very long time – Bruce Springsteen, Crosby, Stills and Nash, Madness, Nick Cave, Spinal Tap, Tom Jones, Status Quo and Tony Christie.

It seemed to reinforce the first words of this piece – good music lasts.

And nobody knows that better than Sonny Knowles.

CHAPTER 1

Liberties Boy

They don't play handball in Chancery Lane any more. Today, this little street in Dublin's Liberties is home to trendy offices where architects, accountants and public relations consultants ply their trade, slipping out occasionally for a 'skinny latte' in the nearby Radisson four star hotel on Golden Lane.

It was a lot different when I spent the first seven years of my life there in the early 1930s. Then the men and the bigger boys played handball against the wall of Dockrell's Timber Yard while we youngsters engaged in endless games of 'Relieveo', skipping and chasing around. It was a noisy, bustling, busy place, inhabited by some 50 families who lived in a row of tenement houses.

Chancery Lane is steeped in history. It was part of The Liberties, an area of mediaeval Dublin which lay outside the walls of the city and not therefore under the jurisdiction of Dublin Corporation. It was divided into parishes named after Irish saints like Patrick, Brigid and Kevin, and was ruled by a number of Masters, including the Archbishop of Dublin, who enforced the law and collected taxes. The Archbishop lived in St. Sepulchre's, which was on the site of Kevin Street Barracks, just around the corner from where we lived.

Families have lived in Chancery Lane for more than 800 years and the street has appeared on maps of Dublin since 1230. It was the site of the church of St. Michael le Pole, which was rediscovered in the 1980s, and also home to tradesmen and their families. The most renowned resident of Chancery Lane was probably John Carpenter, who was born on our street in 1729 and went on to become the Archbishop of Dublin. He became famous for attacking corruption among Dublin clergy and for preaching against drunkenness. Somewhere at the other end of the social spectrum was Roseanne (also known as 'Biddy') Slicker who kept a lodging house for prostitutes at No. 25. Frank Duff, founder of the Legion of Mary, visited the house in 1922 and persuaded the girls living there to go on a retreat to Baldoyle. The 25 'Biddys' travelled out together in a charabanc and never returned because Frank Duff found them 'superior accommodation' at a house in Harcourt Street, which a few years earlier, had been a hiding place for Michael Collins.

We lived at No. 37 Chancery Lane – Tommy Knowles (my Daddy), Mary (my Mammy), Betty, Bridie and Patsy (my sisters), Mick and Harry (my brothers) – and myself, Thomas 'Sonny' Knowles. You went in through a communal hall door and climbed three flights of stairs to get to our 'two per front' flat, which boasted a large 'Drawing Room' looking out onto the lane and another room at the back. At the top of the stairs was a landing, which we put to good use as our kitchen. By day the house was a hive of activity as Mammy looked after endless washing and cooking, slipping out to the local shops to buy groceries or to the lane to chat with her neighbours. The flat was heated by open fires and we bought coal, slack, kindling and sometimes turf, which we had to carry up the three flights of stairs. Fuel was expensive and we used it sparingly. The most modern amenities in the flat were electricity and town gas, which enabled us to cook meals on a gas stove on the landing. There was no bathroom and we had to use an outdoor toilet in the yard or chamber pots if we needed 'to go' at night. We washed ourselves from a cold tap, except on Saturday nights when the big iron bath would be placed in the middle of the back room and Mammy would boil up kettles of hot water so that we could all have a bath and be nice and clean for Mass on Sunday. In the evening we would say the Family Rosary, although we kids often managed to 'escape' the ritual by being absent at play or on an errand. Afterwards the entire appearance of the flat would change as we converted the two rooms into sleeping areas. We had several settee beds which would be pulled out and made up for the night. The girls slept in the front room and the boys in the back. I was very young at the time and I don't quite remember what sleeping arrangements my Daddy and Mammy made for themselves but they must have managed some privacy because they produced the six of us.

It was a happy house – boisterous and noisy at times but always full of life. We played games in the street outside or went to 'The Bano' near St. Patrick's Park after school, where they gave us hot cocoa and buns. Playing football on the street was against the law and so was 'cycling three abreast'. You could get arrested if you were caught by a policeman.

Sometimes we would have a visit from my maternal grandfather Mick Dunne and his wife Mary. Mick worked in the Corporation as a binman and had his own horse and cart, which he kept in Winetavern Street and which he looked after with great care and attention. He was a big man with long white whiskers and a moustache. He wore 'garths', which were protective leggings designed to protect carters from rats or mice which were everywhere on the streets of the city. He told us stories about the Black and Tans and the War of Independence which were still fresh in his mind. We were all broken-hearted when he died suddenly in his sleep.

There was an earlier Sonny Knowles. He was my paternal grandfather and a tailor. I am proud to have inherited both his name and his trade. He died tragically during the Black and Tan era when he ventured out of his house during a curfew and was walking down Capel Street when he was shot by soldiers. I don't remember him or the incident but I do remember being told how my father had to go to identify his body.

I am very proud to follow in the family tradition of my father Tommy Knowles who was a musician. He played drums with the leading dance bands of Dublin in the 1930s, such as The Mai Beardshaw Band, Fred Cooper's Orchestra and The Regal Follies Dance Band. These were 'strict-tempo' dance bands similar to that of Victor Sylvester, who was the equivalent of a 'superstar' in England and who played every day on the BBC Radio programme *Music While You Work*. Daddy loved his music and the dance band life and I remember seeing him all 'dickied out' in his dress suit and bow tie and being collected in a motor car to go off to some dance or other. Mammy looked at him with loving pride almost every evening as he prepared for the night's work, his dark curly hair oiled and brushed and him looking every inch a toff. Daddy also worked sometimes in the building trade and later again got a job with Dublin Corporation.

By now our family was growing. Mick, my eldest brother, had got himself a job at Burton's, the tailors who made men's suits to order and sold them through their own shops in Dublin and around the country. Harry had begun to play the trombone and was continuing the family tradition of musicianship, playing with local bands. My sister Betty was at school, Bridie was a toddler and Patsy was still a baby. I had started at Whitefriar Street National School, where my first teacher was Miss McBride and subsequently I was in the class of Bob Edge, a man with whom I developed a great friendship in later years. We learned our ABCs and our sums and worked our way up from Babies to Big Boys to the First Communion Class. We prepared for months for First Confession with Father Roche, and my Mammy helped me with my list of sins, which were mostly made up.

It was then that tragedy struck our family. Daddy, whose work involved many late hours and playing in sometimes draughty halls, contracted pneumonia which was then a very serious illness. After being nursed by Mammy for weeks, he finally succumbed to the illness and died at home at the age of 37, two days before I was due to make my First Holy Communion.

My Communion Day, therefore, is one that I will never forget as it was also the day of Daddy's funeral. With an incredible mixture of emotions, which I was probably too young to really understand, I saw my Daddy buried and then went to join my classmates in Whitefriar Street Church for the Holy Communion Mass. Later in the day, Mammy brought me to visit aunts and uncles and friends, including my Uncle Joseph who lived in Exchange Street near the City Hall. They all gave me presents and money, which the child in me welcomed warmly, but which with hindsight must have been a very strange experience.

Although I was only seven years of age when Daddy died, I remember him with love and affection. He was a kind and loving husband and a great father – a quiet, sincere, hard working man whose life centred around his family and his music. I would dearly love to have had him as a father for longer – to learn from him, to share in his music and his life, and to accompany him as he grew into middle age and I grew into adulthood.

But it was not to be.

CHAPTER 2

Drimnagh Days

A good way of learning the Mountains of Ireland is to take a trip around Drimnagh where you will find roads called Mourne, Galtymore, Cooley, Sperrin – and Curlew, which was the location of our home for the next 25 years and more.

Drimnagh is a place of 'ridged lands', which is the translation of the Irish name 'Druimneach'. People have lived there since before the dawn of history and a neolithic funerary bowl found there can still be viewed in the National Museum. The area was captured by Strongbow in 1167 and shortly afterwards it was given to one of his Norman soldiers, Hugh de Barnwell. In this respect Strongbow and I have some connection. He lived in Drimnagh and was married in Christ Church Cathedral in the Liberties; I lived in the Liberties and got married in Drimnagh.

'Our Drimnagh' was however a new and modern housing area

when we arrived there. It was among a number of new suburbs built by Dublin Corporation in the 1930s to meet the housing needs of an expanding city and was a 'twin' for Cabra on the Northside. The Corpo houses built there were known as 'parlour homes' and had a living room, kitchen, parlour, bathroom, toilet and two bedrooms with a garden to the rear. Initially the area was also known as North Crumlin, until postal districts were introduced in the mid 1970s when its own name of Drimnagh became generally accepted. It is a place I came to love and admire, and indeed I have never strayed far from its rows of small but cosy houses. Over the years Drimnagh has produced its share of celebrities and sports stars. Think of Olympic boxing gold medalist, Michael Carruth who boxed for the Drimnagh club and Olympic boxer Phil Sutcliffe, athlete Eamon Coghlan, soccer players Don Givens, Jimmy Holmes, Kevin Moran, Tony Dunne and coach Brian Kerr, actors Gabriel Byrne, Patrick and Emmet Bergin, operatic soprano Patricia Cahill, actor and singer Colm Wilkinson, musicians Sean Potts and Sean Keane of The Chieftains, and politician Alan Dukes to drop just a few names. Wasn't I lucky indeed to be moving into their territory!

It happened like this:

When my Daddy died and left Mammy with six children to rear, our family faced a severe financial crisis and we knew that with just Harry and Mick working, it would be impossible to pay the rent and other household expenses in Chancery Lane. So in the best traditions of Dublin families, my aunts and uncle rallied round. Dublin Corporation was moving people from the tenements to the new suburbs at the time and we were lucky enough to be allocated a house at 142 Curlew Road, Drimnagh. I have no real memory of the day we moved but it must have been a wonderful event for Mammy and my older brothers and sisters. After living all their lives in tenements in the heart of the city, they (and I of course) were moving out 'into the country' to a bright, new housing estate with tree-lined roads, open spaces and modern houses. We had our own bathroom and toilet for the first time, hot running water (no more heating up the big iron bath), our own kitchen with a gas cooker and presses, a living room and our own gardens. We were surrounded by other families who were also moving from the Liberties and the inner city and very soon a new community developed with good neighbours, schools and local amenities – all in a Dublin and in an Ireland which was still recovering from the Economic War that only ended in 1938.

Our house shared one important similarity with the flat in Chancery Lane. It was just as crowded. My uncle Stephen and my aunties Frances and Bríd moved in with us. They were fortunate enough to have jobs and their wages helped us to balance the budget for an extended family. It meant however that our two-bedroom house became home to four adults and six children who were all growing up fairly rapidly.

I can never really fully express the love and appreciation I have for my aunts and uncle. They kept our home going when Mammy passed away and I was just 16. If they had not been there to look after us and take over the role of our parents, we could all have ended up in orphanages and our lives would have been very different indeed.

After the move I was enrolled in Mourne Road Primary School, where to my great and pleasant surprise, my master was Bob Edge who had taught me at Whitefriar Street. He also had moved to Drimnagh and was transferred to the local school. Bob was a splendid teacher, tough at times but always fair. He opened up for me the worlds of reading and writing, of maths, geography, history and the Irish language. We remained friends long after our ways parted at school. It was here that I prepared for my Confirmation, having moved from Bob's class to Mr. McDevitt and Mr. Walsh. Confirmation was taken very seriously in the school and we learned page after page of the Catechism by heart, answering questions like 'Who Made the World?' and 'Who is God?' with great certainty. It was much later in life that I realised that these questions have challenged the intellects of even the greatest philosophers and theologians. The object of all this learning was to be prepared for the Bishop's Examination. Before we could be confirmed, the Archbishop of Dublin would visit the school to make sure that we were well versed in our Christian Knowledge. He could ask you any question from the Catechism, so you had to know it all. When he did come to the school however, he asked only simple questions and moved on before anyone had a chance to answer in full – or embarrass the teacher. There was also a lot of talk about the Bishop giving you a 'box in the face' during the Confirmation ceremony to prove that you were a 'strong and perfect Christian', but on the day he just tapped his finger on our cheeks.

Another big challenge at National School was the Primary Certificate Examination. Now long abolished, this was a formal written exam undertaken by 12 to 14-year-olds, a bit like the infamous '11-Plus' in Britain. You had to do sums, correct wrong spellings, know the mountains and rivers of Ireland and a lot more besides. It terrified thousands of young boys and girls because, if you did not pass, you could not get into Secondary School. As matters turned out, I escaped the Primary Examination completely. A teachers' strike called by the INTO took place that year and the exam was cancelled. I presume that we all passed by default – but I was not very worried as my future had already been determined by Mammy and my aunties and uncle.

I was to be a tailor.

Joe Duffy ...
'Sonny by Name –
Sunny by Nature'

'Sonny by name, sunny by nature', is my enduring impression of Ireland's best loved singer.

I had always loved Sonny, back from when I worked in Padbury Advertising in Baggot Street, Dublin and came across his album, *The Wind in My Hands* – the one with Sonny precariously sailing single handed across Howth Harbour.

Even during my college years, my three favourite performers were Leonard Cohen, Neil Young and Sonny Knowles.

And you know what? All three of them are still going strong.

When I first became a producer on the Gay Byrne Radio show in 1991, I wanted Sonny to feature. After all, the most popular radio programme in the country should surely feature the most popular entertainer.

So when I realised that Sonny's 60th birthday was approaching, I decided to think big and go for a surprise broadcast.

Immediately the plan swung into operation, Sheila, Sonny's wife, was contacted. She was quickly roped in and even came up with a cod word for our frequent phone conversations if Sonny happened to answer the phone!

I don't think any household ever got as many phone calls from the 'curtain maker in Hickeys' – but we managed to pull ourselves together and keep the secret.

The next step was to give the 'King of Cabaret' his proper carriage.

We enlisted the help of Dublin Bus and secured their open topped double decker that has carried such luminaries as Jack Charlton, Barry McGuigan and Stephen Roche.

Not only did we get the bus but also it was beautifully decked out in tributes to Sonny. We also arranged for a host of his showbiz friends to assemble at our regular Gay Byrne show outside broadcast venue in North Earl Street.

As the programme lasted only two hours, we had to plan a military style operation to surprise Sonny, get him on the bus and transport him in regal form to North Earl Street.

Of course the Gardaí came on board. I – with Sheila's connivance – surprised Sonny as he nurtured a boiled egg. He was completely gob smacked – live on air.

Luckily Sheila had a decent outfit ready for her husband to jump into – after all, a former tailor always has to look his best.

Along with many of his neighbours, fans and friends from Perrystown, we bundled Sonny on to the top deck of the open top bus.

Unfortunately we forgot about the telephone wires in Sonny's cul–de-sac, which were sheared in two by the double decker. But from then on, it was plain sailing, as the Garda outriders led us down through Patrick Street, Dame Street and the full length of O'Connell Street, before circling back to the junction of North Earl Street.

It was a triumphant journey, fit for a king.

Massive crowds had at this stage gathered for Sonny's arrival and we had a great 60 minutes of entertainment from his old pals like Sil Fox and Dickie Rock.

But the most poignant moment came when we did a linkup with his son Gary in Australia, a genuine moment of connection between father and son.

Gay, of course, loved it all as he sat back in studio – so much so that he played highlights on the following Friday's *Late Late Show.*

That for me began an enduring and lifelong personal relationship with Sonny and Sheila.

They were there for the christening of my three children in 1995 and we all joined with a nation's concern when Sonny went through his health difficulties.

Indeed when Sonny went through his biggest health hurdle a few years ago, a chance phone call from a concerned fan unleashed an avalanche of contributors to *Liveline*. The next 75 minutes were just full of memories of Sonny, including the wonderful story of the time when he played in the divided Cold War city of Berlin.

As Sonny sang on the western side of the Berlin Wall, the communist authorities complained about the noise levels. This generated the immortal headline back in Ireland – 'Reds wail at the Sonny set'.

There will be many more Sonny sets and people will be wailing – but for more!

CHAPTER 3

Making Suits and Music

I t came as no surprise that my family wanted me to get a trade which would guarantee me well paid work for the rest of my life. And it was no surprise either that the trade they chose for me was tailoring. My grandfather, the first Sonny Knowles, was a tailor by trade, Mick worked in Burton's and Uncle Stephen was at Dolcis Shoe Company in Henry Street. And sure weren't we all born within a stone's throw of Tailor's Hall in High Street, the only remaining Dublin Guild Hall, which dates back to 1796?

I was far from being an enthusiastic young apprentice. Even at the age of 15 my sights were set on a career in music – and I had already taken a step or two in that direction. As a young teenager I enrolled in the Dance and Singing Club run by Molly Coulihan in Franshaw House on Crumlin Road, which was owned by the O'Byrne family. You had to pass an audition to get in and I went along with my pal John Dawson. He sang *Poor Ol' Joe*, a Paul Robeson song and with great ambition I sang *The Holy City*, a song I had learned at home and which was later a big number for Brendan Bowyer and the Royal Showband. We were both accepted.

Molly taught us a few songs and a few dance steps and before long, we were putting our newly acquired skills to profitable use in the *Young Talent on Parade* shows at the Queen's Theatre in Pearse Street. You went along and put your name down and got the chance to perform in front of an audience with a lot of other kids who did Irish dances, recitations, Shirley Temple impersonations or sang songs. The top prize was 30 shillings (about €2), second prize was £1 (€1.30) and third prize was 15 shillings (about €1). On one of my first performances I managed to win the top prize and ran home to my mother bursting with pride. She gave me back a half crown (around 20c) to spend on myself. This really encouraged me, so I went back a few times, giving a different name on each occasion and I won a few more prizes. As a result, I probably had several 'stage names' before I was 16.

With all this activity I hardly noticed that the Second World War had been raging in Europe. It began in 1939, the year that we moved from Chancery Lane to Drimnagh, and ended when I was in my final year at Primary School. In Ireland, the War was called 'The Emergency' and because De Valera had declared us to be neutral, we escaped the worst of its effects. Food, however, was rationed and we were issued with a Ration Book for each member of the family, which entitled us to a certain amount of butter, sugar and tea every week. It was usually not enough to go round and families started to drink cocoa or a type of concentrated coffee essence which was sold as 'Irel'. Some other commodities such as coal were in short supply but we managed pretty well. The danger of bombing was always present and indeed some bombs did fall on Dublin. The most serious bombing was on the North Strand where many people were killed. As a protection against a possible gas attack, every citizen, young and old, was issued with a gas mask which came in a solid cardboard box. It was a peculiar contraption made from rubber with large glass goggles and a filter at mouth level through which you could safely breathe. I remember getting fitted for my gas mask at The Bano. They were never used of course because the threatened gas attacks never took place but we kept our gas masks safely in Curlew Road and we would often take them out and play with them when the adults were not around. The Government also set up the Local Defence Force (LDF) as a voluntary army reserve and my brother Harry joined up. He got a uniform and went off on training exercises. Later the LDF became the FCA and was known in Drimnagh as the Free Clothes Association because you got a uniform and a good pair of boots when you joined.

Meanwhile of course, I had a job to look after. Dublin at the time was home to scores of tailoring factories making clothing for both men and women. Polykoff's was among the largest and most successful and was located on the Canal between Rialto and Herberton Bridge in a large factory which was once an aircraft hangar. The English owners came here during the Economic War to supply the Irish market and kept the plant going throughout The Emergency. In those days of fuel shortages, the male workers at the plant would dig turf in the

Dublin Mountains to supply the Polykoff furnaces. The building also had a connection with boxing and was used as a venue for championships before the National Stadium was built. Going to work on my first day was quite daunting. The place seemed huge to me, bustling with people. I am not so sure just how many people worked there but I remember that my time card number was 624. My pal Esmonde Coughlan also joined the company around the same time. He has immaculate handwriting and was quickly dispatched to work in the office (and later be promoted to management) while I headed for the factory floor.

Tailoring was a highly respected trade requiring great skill on the part of the tradesmen and women. It was a 'job for life' and men tended to remain with the same employer throughout their careers. Securing an apprenticeship was not easy – the Trade Unions liked to keep it in the family, so you had to be recommended by a family member who was also in the Trade Union. Luckily for me, Uncle Stephen had the necessary qualifications. Apprentices were taught the basic skills of the trade – how to thread a needle, how to master the various hand stitching techniques like back stitching, herringbone stitching and felling. As they advanced, the apprentices learned how to make button holes by hand, how to use wadding to pad out a suit and finally pattern-making and cutting, which was the most difficult task of all because if you were not perfectly accurate the entire suit could be ruined. Apprentices who attended classes at the Tech had to make a complete hand-stitched suit before they could pass their exams. At Polykoff's we made men's suits throughout the year, overcoats in the Summer and light sports jackets in the Winter, so when it was sunny and warm we were making clothes for the Winter stock and when there was snow on the ground we were making jackets which would be in the shops during the following Summer.

I liked Polykoff's – the place and the people – but I never warmed to the trade of tailoring. It did however have its compensations, like a weekly wage packet which began at 6s10p (about 50p) per week and went up steadily to £1.4s (about €1.10) for a five-day week during which we worked from 8am to 6pm Monday to Friday. We also had the opportunity of working on some Saturdays at time and a half. The trade was divided into specialist skills such as a cutter, shaper, trimmer, fitter or chopper-out. My first job was marking out button holes, then I became a shaper. In truth however, my heart was never in it and I was just marking time until I could 'come out' of my apprenticeship and become a fully-fledged tailor.

Polykoff's also gave me my first real sporting opportunity. I was never that interested in soccer or GAA but when I started working, I dropped down to Polykoff's Boxing Club and did some sparring and gym work. I would be telling a lie however if I suggested that this is where my talents lay. I enjoyed it for a while but as I got bigger, the boxing gloves got tighter and getting punched got more painful. I soon realised that I was never going to be a boxing champion. The experience did however encourage an interest in boxing which has remained with me all my life. I got to know some of Ireland's greatest amateur boxers such as Steve Coffey, Frankie Downes, heavy-weight and overall gentleman Tommy Bruce and Paddy Cahill who was to be groomsman at my wedding. Another boxing friendship that has endured is with Tony 'Socks' Byrne, captain of the Irish boxing team at the Melbourne Olympics at which Ronnie Delany won his famous Gold Medal. A native of Drogheda, Tony, who was the Irish lightweight champion, won a Bronze Medal at those Olympics, one of five medals won by the small Irish team. He proudly carried the Irish flag at the Opening Ceremony and is today commemorated by a life-size statue which is on public display in his native Drogheda. He later emigrated to Canada, where he runs a heavy equipment company, but we stay in touch on a regular basis. Fred Teidt, another great Dublin boxer, won a Silver Medal in the same Olympics but experts later agreed that he should have won the Gold.

In my later life as an entertainer, I got to know the great Barry McGuigan, whose father Pat McGeegan (he changed the spelling for showbiz purposes), was the lead singer with The Big Four, a highly successful band in the Sixties. Boxing remains one of my interests and I like to go along to the National Stadium on the South Circular Road, which over the years has hosted not only some great tournaments but also some great concerts featuring (among others) Louis Armstrong, Cliff Richard and Leonard Cohen.

While I have never been a great supporter of other sports teams, I did admire and follow individual players such as David Parks who played for Bohemians and Shamrock Rovers and whose father Frank was an accomplished trumpet player and vocalist.

Music remained at the centre of my life and I envied Harry and his ability to play the trombone. He suggested that I take up an instrument and although we had an upright piano at home, I opted for the clarinet. One of the happiest days of my life up to that point was when Harry presented me with a brand new Boosey and Hawkes B flat clarinet from Waltons. The instrument was completely new to me and rather strange, but I knew from listening to great players, like Sid Phillips and Benny

Goodman, that it made a beautiful sound. I talked to Jimmy O'Keeffe, a friend at Polykoff's about learning to play and he suggested that I join the Post Office Workers Brass and Reed Band, which was one of many bands then thriving in Dublin. Some, like the ITGWU Band, were attached to Trade Unions and provided members with a social activity, a musical education and the opportunity to lead their fellow workers in parades. With some apprehension I went along to the Post Office Band rehearsal with Jimmy and was given a warm welcome. My first lessons were in the Learners' Section where I learned how to hold the clarinet and master the finger positions, how to make notes by correctly blowing across the reed and then how to play the scale of C. I practiced a lot at the classes and at home, determined to make my lips strong in order to improve the tone of the notes. Harry suggested that I should also learn to read music, so I enrolled in the Dublin School of Music at Chatham Row where Sean O'Keeffe was my teacher. There I learned the theory of music and how to read quavers and semi-quavers and intervals and keys. It was a new and strange language, but one that I loved and picked up fairly quickly. Between the band and the School of Music, I spent almost all of my spare time playing the clarinet. The Post Office Band rehearsed every week and we learned to play marches, hymns and classical pieces. We were invited to play in churches for special ceremonies and to participate in the St. Patrick's Day and other parades. It was a great feeling to march down O'Connell Street in uniform playing Irish marches like *Let Erin Remember the Days of Old* or *O'Donnell Abu*. The band also played concerts in halls or on bandstands around Dublin. I remember playing in St. Stephen's Green, St. Anne's Park in Raheny and on Bray Seafront, when our programme would include pieces like the overtures to

Rossini's *The Thieving Magpie*, Von Suppe's *Poet and Peasant* or selections from the Gilbert and Sullivan operettas.

As I became more competent on the clarinet, I got my first professional gigs. They were largely in bands playing for tennis club 'hops' at Oulton Road or Sandymount. Often I would play with Harry, who was a member of Pat Moran's Four Piece which was very popular at these 'hops'. This experience gave me a taste for playing at dances and I began to go along to dance halls, just to listen to the bands that played there, such as Johnny Butler, Pat Moran, Joe Coughlan and Mick Delahunty.

I was now coming to the end of my apprenticeship at Polykoff's and I decided that having secured the trade of tailoring, I would bid it goodbye.

From then onwards, music was to be my life.

CHAPTER 4

Sheila

When it came to dances, I was not always on the stage. Dancing was big in the Dublin of the Fifties with a string of ballrooms spread around the city from the National and Ierne on Parnell Square to the Crystal and Ballerina in the city centre to the Olympia and Palm Court in Aungier Street to the Four Provinces in Harcourt Street. The ballrooms were open every night and thousands of young people went dancing five nights a week.

Among them was Sheila O'Shea.

We met, of course, at a dance. Not in one of the major ballrooms, but in Drimnagh School. I went along with Jack Short and, as was our practice on such occasions, we 'shifted' two birds – Sheila and her friend Alice Heavey. We had 'scored' with girls on a regular basis previously and would be rewarded with 'a court' or maybe a date or two. But until then neither of us was 'going steady.'

This time it was different – very different. We ended up marrying the two girls.

You might say that it was a case of love at first sight, but I don't remember it like that. We just got on well, Jack and Alice, Sheila and I. We went to dances together and to the pictures and later we joined An Óige and went hiking and cycling in Wicklow. Jack and I became keen hikers and hostellers. We would cycle to hostels in Glendalough or Aughavanna or maybe up to Mellifont in Co. Louth. Sometimes we would get the bus to Enniskerry and hike from there up to Enniscree or along the Wicklow Way in our hobnail boots. Once we went off to Aberystwyth in North Wales. The girls would usually come with us but they were not allowed by their parents to stay overnight in the hostels, so they only joined us on the day trips.

Sheila lived on Clonard Road in Crumlin and went to school at St. Agnes National School, Loreto on the Green and Ard Scoil Eanna, a Gaelscoil known locally as the 'shilling a week school' because it charged fees. She had twin sisters, Mary and Ann, who were seven years younger. Sheila loved sewing as a youngster and it was again no surprise when she too took up tailoring. She worked for Hymie Michaels, a company which made ladies clothing at Ormond Quay.

By then we had all learned to dance – because you had to be able to do the Foxtrot, the Quickstep and the Old Time Waltz if you were to have any chance of shifting a bird at a hop. You also needed to be able to jive, even though rock'n'roll had not yet arrived. We went to a lot of dances together but when I was playing in a band, Sheila would go dancing to some other hall. She did not want to be looking up at me all night on the stage and I certainly did not want to be looking down at her dancing with other fellas.

I don't remember ever asking Sheila if we could 'go steady' – it just happened and I think you could say the same about Jack and Alice. Nor do I remember getting down on one knee and asking her to marry me. But I must have proposed at some stage. We got engaged on 17th June 1955 when we went into town together and bought the engagement ring in Grafton Street in a jewellers where Marks and Spencer now stands. Sheila looked at a whole lot of rings and was having some difficulty making up her mind but she finally plumped for a solitaire, mainly, she says, because the sales assistant kept putting it back in the tray and didn't seem to want to part with it. I was keeping a keen eye on the proceedings of course – trying to make out the figures on the little price tags. Later we celebrated by going to a dress dance in Clery's Ballroom.

We were married by Father O'Sullivan in St. Agnes Church in Crumlin on 1st June 1957, the year I became a fully-fledged professional musician. Jack Short, of course, was my Best Man and Paddy Cahill, whom I knew from my boxing days, was the Groomsman. Sheila's twin sisters Mary and Ann were Brides-maids. I remember being entranced when I saw Sheila arrive by my side at the altar in the beautiful wedding dress which she had made herself and which I was not allowed to see until that moment. It was a lovely Summer day and we had the reception in a marquee erected in the garden of Sheila's family home in Clonard Road. There was quite a gathering of musicians including Earl Gill, members of Dick Cahill's Band, my brother Harry, and Chris Doyle, who was a great singer. They all contributed to the entertainment and Sheila's Dad, Austin O'Shea, did his party piece singing *The Minstrel Boy*.

We spent our honeymoon in London and naturally we went dancing most evenings to big lavish ballrooms like the Lyceum and the Hammersmith Palais to the music of bands such as Geraldo, Oscar Rabin, Ted Heath with singers Dickie Valentine and Lita Rosa and of course, Joe Loss.

The Joe Loss Band was resident at the Hammersmith Palais and was among the most famous in Europe. A big outfit, it comprised a reed section of five saxes, a brass section of four trumpets and four trombones, a rhythm section of piano, bass, drums and guitar and two vocalists – Rose Brennan and Ross McManus. Some members of the band had Irish connections. Rose Brennan was from Cabra and Ross McManus was the father of Declan Patrick McManus, better known as singer/songwriter Elvis Costello. The lead alto player was Frank Gillespie who hailed from Waterford. My particular interest however was in Bill Brown, the baritone sax player. I had been playing alto sax at the time and I was considering a move to baritone. I listened carefully to Bill Brown who was a magnificent player and I bucked up the courage to ask him if he would give me a lesson as I was taking up the baritone sax. He kindly agreed and the next day we spent an hour together during which he taught me the blowing technique. I don't know if I needed more courage to approach him or to chance taking a music lesson during my honeymoon.

Jack, who was a cabinet maker and builder, and Alice got married that same year and our friendship endured for more than four decades. We met regularly, went on holidays together and ended up living in the same estate in Crumlin where each of us had the same house number. We each lived at No. 27 but on different roads. Sadly, they both died in 2008 within a few weeks of each other. I like to think that they could not bear to be separated from each other and that they are now together in a better place.

We have lived in only one house since we married in 1957. Sheila and I were out for a walk some months before our wedding when we spotted a new housing development at Muckross in Crumlin. The builders had put up a large sign which said: 'A £50 deposit secures any home on this development.' We made up our minds there and then. I nipped back home and got £50 out of a tin box where I had saved up some money and we went straight to the builder and reserved the house which was to be our new home. The house was ready when we got married the following June and we were one of the first couples to move into what was then green fields with just this new housing development. We got the keys on 21st May 1957 – just ten days before the wedding. I was playing in the Shelbourne at the time, usually for dress dances which did not finish until 3am, so it would be 4am before I got home. There was no street lighting after the Submarine Bar about half a mile away and the area was pitch black at night. It was lonely for Sheila who was in the house on her own most nights, so we bought a boxer dog for protection and company. Typically, the dog also had a musical background. He was bred by Alan Beale, a clarinet player in the Theatre Royal Orchestra who was also a successful dog breeder, and was given the name 'Andante Cantabile.' We called him 'Dante' and he lived with us for 15 years. He was a purebred so we were encouraged to bring him to dog shows. This involved first of all going to obedience classes so that he would respond to commands like 'sit', 'stop', 'stay', 'trot' or 'walk'. He became really obedient and if we put food in front of him, he would not start to eat until given permission to do so, even though he would be drooling. Next of course he had to look his best on show days, so there was a lot of grooming to be done. But we were very proud of Dante who won lots of rosettes and prizes during his life.

Our daughter Geraldine was born in February 1959 and our son Gary arrived in April 1960. Having two young babies in the house made a huge difference of course. Sheila's dancing nights were over for a while, although we were always able to find babysitters when we had the chance of going out together. Then I joined the Pacific Showband (about which more later) and I was on the road five nights of the week with rehearsals on the sixth. As a result I was away a lot from home while Geraldine and Gary were growing up and with the benefit of hindsight, I can say that I missed out badly on the great joy of watching and helping children grow from being babies to tots and then young people. Sheila did virtually all the rearing of our first two children and while I tried to do my part, the facts were that the demands of being a full time musician just kept me away from home.

It was a different situation when Aisling was born in 1973. By then I had become a cabaret artiste and I was at home most days and back after gigs at a reasonable hour. As a result, I have more vivid and happy memories of Aisling growing up than I do of Geraldine and Gary.

The children attended local schools and made lots of friends, who would come around to play in the open space in front of our house. We planted two trees on the grass about the same distance apart as goalposts and when they grew they were used for that purpose. They now stand about 30 feet tall but when

Gary or our grandchildren come to visit, they are still used as goalposts in kick-about games.

Gary was a keen footballer from childhood and played with Manor Town United. When he finished school at Greenhills College, all he wanted to do was to play soccer. He was spotted by a scout from West Bromwich Albion and we were approached by John Giles and Eamon Dunphy who wanted to sign him as an apprentice. We were apprehensive about allowing him to go off to England's West Midlands but we were assured that he would be well looked after and that there was a strong Irish presence at the club. In any event wild horses would not have held Gary back from a chance of playing professional soccer in England. 'The Baggies' as West Brom were known were among the oldest clubs in England, having been founded in 1878. The club was a founder member of the Football League in 1888 and won the very first FA Cup. John Giles became player manager at West Brom in 1975, having moved from Leeds where he had a brilliant playing career but was overlooked twice for the job as manager. He had just been named manager of the Irish national team and combined both roles with considerable success. West Brom won promotion to the First Division in 1975 and took seventh place in the First Division in the following year.

Gary came to this well-run and successful club as an apprentice and worked his way up through the reserves to win a number of first team appearances. He developed a good relationship with the player manager and when John Giles decided to return to Ireland and Shamrock Rovers in 1977, Gary came with him – as did Eamon Dunphy. Their dream was to make Shamrock Rovers the first fully professional team in Ireland which could compete effectively in European competitions as well as on the home front. The adventure got off to a great start when Rovers won the FAI Cup in 1978 but in subsequent years success was more elusive and John Giles eventually returned to England, while Eamon Dunphy moved into journalism. Gary was a regular on the Rovers team but of course, soccer was not a full-time profession in Ireland then – nor is it now. Gary married Linda Hearn, his childhood sweetheart at the age of 22 and went off to work at Fujitsu, which had a microchip manufacturing plant in Tallaght. He remained there for a few years but was always on the lookout to improve himself and his career. The opportunity came when he got the chance of working for Fujitsu in Australia and he and Linda decided to take it. One of the biggest shocks Sheila and I ever had was when they told us that they were emigrating. I can tell you that it took the legs from under me. Moving to England or even America would be bad enough – at least they were fairly accessible. Australia however was on the other side of the world and you could not just drop over there for a weekend. Driving Gary and Linda to the airport to catch the first leg of their flight to Perth was one of the most difficult and emotional moments of my life. I felt that I was losing my only son, who was moving to the other side of the Earth – and indeed so did Sheila.

Geraldine meanwhile had also finished her studies at Loreto on Crumlin Road and was working for the accountancy firm of Stokes Kennedy Crowley. She also married at a young age and shortly afterwards, she and her plumber husband Kevin Dunne moved to Kent in England. They never really settled in England however and when Gary invited them out on a holiday to Australia, they loved the place. No sooner were they back home than they were making plans to sell up and to join Gary and Linda in Perth – which, in due course, they did.

Aisling, our baby, went into the airline business after doing her Leaving Certificate at St. Paul's. She worked for Ryanair at Stansted Airport near London and while there met her future husband, English-born Rob McMillan. Being in the travel business, Aisling got to fly around a lot and eventually, lo and behold, she and Rob also decided to move to Australia so that today our son, two daughters and five grandchildren all live within a mile or so of each other in Perth.

Their decision to move 'Down Under' has brought them a good life and careers, but for Sheila and me it has been a terrible wrench. Over the past 20 years or so, we have managed to get out to see them about every 18 months or so and they have visited us in Dublin. For a long time it was easy enough to go. I was doing very well on the cabaret scene and whenever we had a gap in the diary, I could just call up the travel agent and get on the next available plane. Illness, however, has made travel more difficult and it is now quite an effort to make the long journey to Perth, although it is of course always most rewarding to get to see our children and grandchildren. Gary's son Raymond (23) now lives and works in Abu Dhabi while their daughter Haley is aged 16 and still at college. Geraldine and Kevin have two boys, Kenny (25) and Alan (23) and a daughter Lorna (21).

Sheila and I thought long and hard about moving to Australia to be with the family but at the time my cabaret career was flying and I knew that it would be very difficult to build another career as an entertainer in Australia. Even if I did that, it would involve long journeys and nights on the road. We decided therefore to stay in Dublin, but with the great benefit of hindsight, I often think that moving to Australia ten years ago, being with my family and watching our grandchildren grow up, would have been the preferable option. I could not foresee then, of course, what twists and turns life would take.

As showbusiness lives go, ours has been quiet, peaceful and relatively uneventful. While I am well known to audiences and the Irish public, I have never seen myself as a star or a celebrity. Most of the time, we have lived quietly in Crumlin, taking a few holidays every year in Spain and socialising with our friends. We have been blessed with many good friends who have remained close to us over many years. Some are in the entertainment business, but most are not. Sheila's mother Eileen lived with us for 14 years until she passed away 17 years ago and her presence added enormously to our sense of family. Sheila loves life and accompanies me to many gigs and social events. Even when our children were growing up, she would always manage to find babysitters.

Outside of music I have never been a great hobby person. I tried playing golf a few times but I was both hopeless and disinterested. I was more likely to enjoy the scenery of the golf course than to concentrate on putting the ball in the hole. For some strange reason, it also seemed to pour rain whenever I went out on the golf course. Maybe the Man Above was trying to tell me something. Nor was I ever a DIY man. Indeed, I could not drive a nail into a plank to save my life. Music was and remains my one and only interest apart from Sheila and our family – and both have brought me wonderful rewards.

Swinging in Kinsale with Paddy Cole

Sonny Knowles is a great favourite at the Kinsale Jazz Festival, which takes place over the October Bank Holiday in Actons Hotel. It provides a 'fringe' for the big Guinness Jazz Festival 'down the road' in Cork and it attracts musicians and listeners who like their jazz to be swinging and traditional.

The band includes legendary Cork musicians such as Joe Mac, Jack Brierley, Marco Petrassi and Billy Crosbie and we are often augmented by visitors from overseas. Indeed the stage can get so crowded, that if you step forward to play a solo, you might have difficulty regaining your place in the line.

Sonny has been part of our happy band for the past 15 years. He began playing the baritone sax but these days he prefers to play alto, which he says is lighter to carry. It is when he puts down the sax and picks up the microphone to sing however, that Sonny comes into his own. It only takes the opening bars of a song for him to have the audience on its feet and in the palm of his waving hand.

It has always been thus, for as long as I know him as a musician, singer and entertainer. Our first contact was when we were both young sax players, learning our trade. I was with the Maurice Lynch Orchestra from my home town of Castleblayney and Sonny was in the Earl Gill and Neil Kearns Orchestras. We both sat on our seats, playing arrangements of the big band music of Glen Miller and Tommy Dorsey, and only rarely did we get a chance to sing.

When the showbands revolutionised dancing, Sonny joined The Pacific and I went to The Capitol. We both toured the country in orbits that occasionally crossed and when we did, it was always a pleasure. From those early days, Sonny and I began a close friendship which has endured over the decades.

When the showband era began to fade, Sonny was already a big cabaret star in his native Dublin. Indeed he pioneered the cabaret scene, building up an enormous fan base in venues like the Drake Inn and the Tudor Room. He seemed to be singing everywhere and was much loved by his army of fans. So, when I was asked to do a two-week residency at the Braemor Rooms, I knew where to look for a guest artiste. Sonny joined us for the shows, which were a huge success and we had a great time playing Dixieland, singing a few songs and recreating the sound of Billy Vaughan on two saxes.

Sonny is a highly talented professional musician and a consummate entertainer and he brings those unique talents to the fore when we all sing and swing together by the sea in Kinsale.

CHAPTER 5

Swinging and Singing

My musical ambitions in the early 1950s were strictly in the realm of playing an instrument. I had made good progress on the clarinet and then took up the alto saxophone, which was broadly similar but required a slightly different technique. And, of course, it produced a very different sound. Classical and dance band players also use different techniques and I got some very useful tips on playing 'the modern way' from band leader Joe Coughlan and Abe Cohen who was in the Neil Kearns Orchestra. The 'sax' was the cool instrument of its day. It provided the core of the reed section with alto, tenor and baritone saxes playing in harmony. The instrument, or rather series of instruments, was invented by a Belgian-born clarinet player, Adolfe Saxe in 1841 as an instrument that would be louder than the clarinet in brass bands. His B flat and E flat saxes are by far the most popular with jazz and dance band musicians but he also invented saxophones pitched in C and F which are used mainly in classical music.

I grew up as an avid admirer of the sax, particularly as it sounded in the big swing bands of Glen Miller and Tommy Dorsey. It was as an alto sax player that I made my debut as a serious professional musician with the Johnny Butler Orchestra in the Ballerina Ballroom and I also played the instrument alongside my brother Harry on trombone in a band led by Pat Moran at the Four Provinces Ballroom.

My first big opportunity came from the legendary Earl Gill who was then the youngest bandleader in Ireland at the age of 21. He had already built a reputation as a fine trumpet player and musical arranger and had led bands which played in the Shelbourne Hotel and the big ballrooms. I sat in with him in 1959 in a one-off band which played at the Irish premiere of the film *Darby O'Gill and the Little People*. He got the gig because the Theatre Royal Orchestra was on holidays. The film had a star-studded cast which included Janet Munro, Sean Connery, the great Beckett actor Jack McGowran and our own Jimmy O'Dea. Walt Disney himself and most of the cast turned up to the premiere and the party which followed and it was a great thrill to do some serious 'people spotting'.

Earl Gill was to have a huge influence on my musical career and he remains one of my heroes. We have been great friends over the years and I am delighted that he still plays the trumpet as well as ever. Towards the end of the Fifties, Earl had become aware of the new showbands which were making waves in many parts of the country. He was putting a new band together to play at the Palm Court Ballroom in Aungier Strteet and was recruiting young musicians. He had already hired Jim Farley, another great musician and long time friend, to play lead alto sax and was on the lookout for a second alto player. I was recommended to him and I landed the job. Playing with musicians of this calibre was a big move up the ladder for me and the initial rehearsals were a little terrifying. We would be presented with sheet music and expected to sight read and play it straight off. There would be several rehearsals, of course, before we played the arrangement in public but we would nevertheless be expected to give a good account of ourselves at the first reading. Luckily I had been a diligent student in the theory classes at Chatham Street and I had gained useful experience playing with the Post Office Band so I was able to hold my own with a very talented bunch of musicians. I sat alongside Jim Farley, who was an excellent reader, and we struck up a sound musical relationship.

This Earl Gill Band had a lineup of four saxes, trumpet, trombone, piano, bass, drums and vocalist Dick Dorney. We played some of the standard arrangements from the Glen Miller, Tommy Dorsey and Count Basie songbooks, which could be bought at Waltons in Parnell Street or from May's on St. Stephen's Green. What marked us out from other bands however was the way in which Earl could take an arrangement and switch it around, repeating some sections, transposing others or dropping some altogether. It made the arrangements sound fresh and gave the band a fresh and exciting sound.

We played four nights a week at the Palm Court and I was a happy camper playing second alto and listening to Dick sing the hit songs of the day. While I had sung a song or two in my time, most notably *The Holy City* for Molly Coulihan and a few numbers in the Queen's Theatre talent shows, that was in my boy soprano days. I also tried singing in a few choirs but soon lost interest. Once my voice broke, I didn't bother singing again as my musical energies were focused on playing the clarinet and sax.

Then one evening, when I was minding my own business in the front row of the band during a rehearsal, Earl came up to me and said, 'Sonny – do you sing?'

'I think I do a bit – but it's a long time since I sang anything,' I replied.

'Well – what do you know?'

'I think I know "Down by the Riverside"'

'OK, we'll give it a try.'

And with that, Earl started working out a Dixieland arrangement of the good old potboiler – and I started my singing career. For several weeks after that, I would pop up out of my seat once in a night to sing *Down by the Riverside* and that was the limit of my vocalising until eventually Earl asked me: 'Sonny – would you consider learning another song?'

Which of course I did – and very soon I was the second vocalist in the band. Unlike the clarinet and sax playing, I never had formal singing lessons. I just took a chance and kept going – and I am still taking a chance and going strong today.

Playing with Earl, and later with other bands in Dublin, was a great experience for a young musician but it was also hard work. We were on stage at least four nights a week doing sets that ran from 9pm to 1am or 2am and if we played for a dress dance, it would run until 4am. Over at the Shelbourne for instance, the regular dancing hours were 9pm to 3am. Even Bruce Springsteen would not do those kinds of marathon gigs today.

My 'Daddy', Tommy Knowles, all dressed up for a dance.

Frank Cooper and his Ritz Dance Band with my Daddy sitting at the drums.

Dick Cahill's Band. That's me on sax next to the drummer.

Jimmy Edwards, the British actor, playing trombone with the Earl Gill Orchestra at the Shelbourne Hotel ballroom.

Together with members of the Earl Gill Orchestra, I get to meet Count Basie.

The late Charlie Deveney, myself, Rock Fox and Earl Gill blowing at a jazz session.

The Neil Kearns Orchestra on the diving board at Butlins's Holiday Camp where we were resident for a Summer season. I am in the front row with my clarinet.

The Pacific Showband. We handed out thousands of these postcard pictures at dances.

Dermot O'Brien and The Clubmen. I am squatting on the right with my baritone sax.

Our Wedding Day. Sheila and I with Paddy Cahill, Jack Short, Ann and Mary O'Shea.

*Happy Bride and Groom.
With Sheila on our Wedding Day.*

*Sheila, Gary, Geraldine,
Aisling and myself pose
for a family 'snap'.*

Singing in 'Holiday Hayride' which starred Jack Cruise.

On the cabaret scene.

With Frank Ifield at the Drake Inn.

With Acker Bilk at the Drake Inn.

With the great Muhammad Ali.

With Hugo Quinn of the Clipper Carlton.

With boxing legend Henry Cooper.

Singing at an international Song Contest in Split.

On stage in Las Vegas.

Opposite page: Playing with my brother Harry in the Bobby Lambe Big Band. We are second and third from the right of the front row.

Hitting a Six at a charity Cricket Match in 1983.

Receiving my VATS 'Hall of Fame' Award from Jimmy Ryan.

With Roly Daniels

With Dickie Rock, Joe Cahill and Joe Duffy

With Sheila- the love of my life.

Write it down- it's a good one'...sharing a joke with Hal Roach.

Announcing our Engagement!

Various conversations would take place between band members during a long dance. On one occasion I was playing with Earl and also rehearsing with another band leader for an RTÉ Christmas show. During a break between numbers, Earl asked me how I was getting on with the man in question.

'OK,' I replied, 'but he is a bit of a bully.'

'I always found him to be a nice guy,' replied Earl.

'But you were talking to him as leader to leader. He is talking to me as leader to foot soldier,' I retorted.

One word borrowed another and before we knew what was happening, we were both standing up shouting at each other while the band behind us played away. When the number ended, Earl was still furious. He walked over to the microphone and instead of announcing the next dance, he told an astonished crowd, 'I don't know – I always found him to be a nice guy.'

The Dublin musicians tended to know each other well and many lasting friendships were formed. Abe Cohen was particularly good to me, giving me lessons and looking out for opportunities. He played with the Neil Kearns Orchestra which was resident at the Gresham and when a vacancy arose for a lead alto player there, he mentioned my name to Neil. I was happy of course playing at the Palm Court but I knew that I would not be promoted to lead alto as long as Jim Farley was in the band – and he showed no signs of wanting to move on. Neil invited me to try out and I got the job.

During the Summer, the Neil Kearns Orchestra was resident in Butlin's Holiday Camp at Mosney, Co. Meath, just 25 miles north of Dublin. Built in 1948 as part of a network of Butlins camps throughout the UK and Ireland, it was a huge holiday attraction for families from all over the country, who slept in chalets and participated in a very wide range of activities organised by the famous Red Coats. At that time, more than 2,800 campers and 4,000 day visitors arrived at the Co. Meath venue every week to enjoy the sea air, the amusements, the fun park, the bingo hall, the indoor and outdoor swimming pools, the bars, restaurants – and the ornate ballroom.

As resident entertainers we lived in the holiday camp for the months of July and August, not able to get home to our families because we did not have motor cars and in any event we were working almost non-stop. The band would of course play for the tea time and evening dances but we would also be needed for the Talent Competition, Glamorous Grandmother, Mosney Princess, Knobbly Knees and a whole list of other contests and events. Even though we had our bed and board and our own chalets, I felt a bit 'handcuffed' up there and worked Mosney for only one season. That was in my second year with Neil – and I never went back.

By now I was getting interested in widening my musical horizons and had a keen interest in the baritone sax. As I said earlier, I had a lesson on the technique of playing the instrument during our honeymoon in London and I was now determined to make the move. The opportunity arose when Earl Gill had an idea for a new sound for his band, which was now resident in the Shelbourne Hotel. Ever the innovator, he decided to substitute an alto with a baritone sax and I was invited to fill the slot. In effect, I played the first alto parts on the baritone and it had the impact of giving the band a new, edgy sound which would be a match for the showbands. He also began to introduce some rock numbers into the programme, particularly if we played at the Mourne Road Hall or a similar venue on a Sunday night. We had also gone to see Brendan Bowyer and the Royal Showband from Waterford who were attracting huge crowds wherever they played and Earl was impressed by the fact that all the musicians stood up. After that, we lost our nice comfortable seats and we stood up too when we played a five-week residency at the Seapoint Ballroom in Salthill.

That period with Earl Gill's band was among the most enjoyable of my musical career. I was surrounded by superb musicians who were great sight readers, arrangers and performers. Apart from Earl, the band included my good friend Jim Farley on lead alto, the late Liam Forrestal on tenor sax, Shay Nolan on trumpet, Wally Spence on trombone, Richie Glynn on drums, Dick Keating on piano, Jack Rogers on bass and Dick Dorney who was lead vocalist. Like most professional musicians of the day, we were all members of the Irish Federation of Musicians and indeed Richie Glynn was a national officer. The 'Fed' was the musicians' trade union and you had to pass an audition to show your competence before you could become a member. Luckily I escaped that particular test as my studies at the Dublin School of Music earned me an exemption. The 'Fed' set minimum rates of pay but of course most of us earned more than the minimum because we were sought after by the band leaders. It also had certain rules governing overseas artistes performing here. If a UK band played in Dublin, Cork, Limerick or other areas where the 'Fed' had members, the promoters were obliged to hire a band of 'Fed' musicians as a warm-up or interval act. This rule also applied in the USA where the Musicians' Union insisted that for every visiting musician (say from Ireland or Britain), an American musician also had to be hired, so we had occasions when a band like our ten piece would be on stage in New York or Chicago and ten American musicians, all dressed in their tuxedos, would just stand around and listen.

My association with the Earl Gill Orchestra also brought me into a musical 'family' which included some of the finest musicians in the Dublin of the Sixties – people like John Curran the sax player and arranger, Johnny Tate trumpeter and talented arranger, Johnny Christopher a most intelligent drummer, Noel Keelehan pianist and arranger, jazz pianist Jim Doherty and singers like Des Smith and Anne Bushnell. We were in demand as backing musicians and singers for showbands who were making records and unknown to their many fans, I sang on hits recorded by people like the Royal and Hilton Showbands, Tommy Drennan, Sean Dunphy and others. We also made radio and TV commercials and jingles, in studios operated by Eamon Andrews and Tommy Ellis.

A most rewarding experience was playing with what is now called the RTÉ Concert Orchestra and was then known as the 'Light Orchestra'. When the scores demanded additional instruments, we would be called in to augment the regular orchestra – either to record music or to play live in places like the O'Connell Hall or the Francis Xavier Hall, where regular broadcasts would be compered by people like Roy Croft or Joe Linnane. You had to be a good musician and sight reader to play at this level and to be able to work with a range of conductors. To this day I am an admirer of orchestra players who can pick up their instruments and play the most intricate and difficult music on first sight.

Some of the musicians who worked on those gigs formed an ad hoc group called 'Family Pride', which sang on radio shows and made an LP. They included John Curran, Johnny Christopher, Anne Bushnell, Pat and Jean O'Reilly and myself, all singing in close harmony and occasionally a cappella. It was a nice warm sound and although the LP did not make it into the charts, it remains one of the projects in which I am proud to have taken part.

My most memorable experience with Earl, however, was when we toured the USA with Ruby Murray in 1959. The Belfast-born singer was then one of the biggest stars in show business this side of the Atlantic. A throat operation in early childhood contributed to her unique singing voice and in 1955 she had no fewer than five records in the charts at the same time including her biggest hit *Softly Softly*, an achievement which has never been equalled – even by The Beatles. She had her own TV show and appeared at the London Palladium with Norman Wisdom. She also appeared in the movie *A Touch of the Sun* with Frankie Howerd and Dennis Price. Ruby's succession of chart hits had petered out by the time we toured with her in 1959 but she was much loved by the Irish in America and was mobbed by fans at packed Irish halls throughout the tour. Sadly in later life, she encountered marital and alcohol problems and died from liver cancer in December 1996 at the age of 61.

That tour was a new and exciting experience for me and, I reckon, for most of the boys in the band. Until then, my only travel as a musician had been to Britain so it was amazing to visit cities like New York, Boston and Philadelphia, to walk through Times Square and Quincy Market, to travel by day in trains, to play new venues every night and to meet hundreds of Irish Americans. We looked forward to our spot on the show, playing standard and original arrangements of dance tunes and then to backing Ruby during her act.

If this was showbiz – I was all for it.

And there were also two more reasons for Sheila and I to be very happy as the Sixties arrived. Our daughter Geraldine was born in 1959 and our son Gary arrived in 1960.

We never thought that it would all change so quickly.

Earl Gill ...
'A Singing Musician'

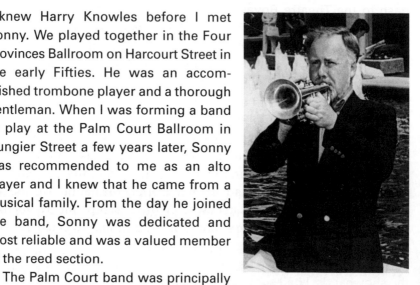

I knew Harry Knowles before I met Sonny. We played together in the Four Provinces Ballroom on Harcourt Street in the early Fifties. He was an accomplished trombone player and a thorough gentleman. When I was forming a band to play at the Palm Court Ballroom in Aungier Street a few years later, Sonny was recommended to me as an alto player and I knew that he came from a musical family. From the day he joined the band, Sonny was dedicated and most reliable and was a valued member of the reed section.

The Palm Court band was principally an instrumental outfit. We had Dick Dorney as our singer but he only sang a few songs during a set. That was the pattern then. Neil Kearns, for instance, had a lady singer who would do just three or four numbers over a night's music. We liked to try out new things and at one stage, Sonny volunteered to sing a Dixieland number. We gave it a try and he sang the same one tune every time we played. Eventually I asked him if he would think about learning another song – and of course he did.

Sonny was in a band I put together for the world premiere of the film *Darby O'Gill and the Little People*, which was screened at the Theatre Royal and was attended by Walt Disney and most of the cast, including Jimmy O'Dea. I had worked hard at arranging music from

Disney films like *Sleeping Beauty, Cinderella* and *Snow White and the Seven Dwarfs* , and we rehearsed the programme over a week. On the day of the premiere, a friend of mine in Ballyfermot asked me if I would do his bread round as he had come down with the flu. I agreed and packed my dress suit in alongside the pan loaves, before heading off around the houses. The round took longer than I expected and I had a dash to the Theatre Royal, which was surrounded by people. The Gardaí were diverting traffic and didn't want to let me through. Eventually they relented and I just managed to get into my tuxedo before it was time to stand in front of the band, smelling, I am sure, of freshly baked bread.

Sonny also toured with our band when we did Summer seasons in Galway. On one memorable occasion, a fierce row broke out in the band bus – an 'elderly' Volkswagen. It became so heated that the driver stopped the bus and ordered everyone out onto the road. We piled out, continuing the argument, until we noticed that the bus was not there anymore. The driver had omitted to apply the handbrake and the vehicle had taken off, on its own, down a steep hill. Never did musicians move as fast as our crew, as we sprinted to catch up with the runaway bus and somehow get to the brakes.

In the early Sixties we became aware of the growing popularity of the showbands. I had some experience playing with Gaye McIntyre in Derry and we also saw The Royal Showband who shared the season with us at Seapoint in Galway. We introduced a few changes into our programme, devising a *South Pacific* sequence, standing up most of the time and even pumping dry ice onto the stage. Sonny also came into his own as a singer as we included more vocal numbers in the set. We would often try these innovations, first in dances out in Perrystown, before we introduced them in the city centre.

When Sonny moved to The Pacific, we went our separate ways. I formed The Hoedowners which played on the showband circuit and Sonny eventually moved into cabaret. We would however occasionally play together in RTÉ orchestras at the National Concert Hall and in Montrose.

Sonny is first and foremost a musician and he brings this musical expertise to his cabaret work. Unlike many singers, he has a technical knowledge of his music, including the keys in which he sings. His musicianship has given him a keen sense of phrasing and timing and he knows how to work with other musicians. He has always been an excellent reader of music, a dedicated instrumentalist and singer and in every sense a true professional.

Most of all he is a sincere and nice man, a great husband to Sheila, father to his children and grandfather. We have been good friends since we first met and I have been privileged to know him.

CHAPTER 6

Showband Days ... and Nights

On Monday 12th April 1954, popular music changed forever. On that day, William John Clifton Haley from Highland Park, Michigan went into the Pythian Temple Studios in New York with his band The Comets and recorded a song called *We're Gonna Rock Around the Clock* for US Decca.

When the record hit the streets, the world stopped and danced.

The record itself only managed to stay in the US charts for a few weeks but it was soon replaced by Haley's second massive hit *Shake, Rattle and Roll* which took the music world by storm. Before very long, the records were being played on sponsored programmes on Radio Éireann and when the film *Rock Around the Clock* arrived in Irish cinemas early in 1955, the whole country went crazy.

Intoxicated by this new refreshing sound, Irish teenagers embraced rock'n'roll with an enthusiasm unknown since the days of the Charleston. They stood up and danced in cinemas where the film was shown and there were instances of mini riots and seats being ripped out. Never had music exercised such a powerful influence on the youth of Ireland who had been raised on a musical diet of crooners and céilí bands.

Bill Haley was soon joined by Fats Domino, Little Richard, Buddy Holly, Gene Vincent, Eddie Cochrane, by a close harmony group called The Platters and then by the great Elvis Presley who was to dominate the music charts for the next few years with records designed to get people jiving – at home, in the streets and, of course, in the dance halls.

This new development was not exactly suited to orchestras like those of Maurice Mulcahy, Mick Delahunty, Brose Walsh, Neil Kearns or our Earl Gill band, which were the mainstay of the ballrooms in the Fifties. We played the latest hits from sheet music arrangements and we sat down throughout the performance, getting to our feet occasionally to play a few bars of *American Patrol* or, for some of us, to sing a song. This pattern was just not suitable for rock'n'roll and soon Earl had us standing up for some numbers when we played in venues like Drimnagh Hall or were 'on the road' during the Summer months in Galway or Limerick. Some bands developed little 'shows' within their sets. They would put away the music stands and mimic the pop stars of the day for a half hour or so while the crowd stopped dancing and stood around to watch. Some say this is where the phrase 'show stopper' originated. Among the first to develop such a show was The Clipper Carlton from

Strabane whose *Jukebox Saturday Night* feature was so popular that they abandoned their music stands altogether and spent the entire set standing up, waving their instruments about, jiving, clapping and dancing as they performed the hit songs of the day. In the beginning, they did not call themselves a showband – that title was first used by a band headed by Dave Glover – but 'The Clippers' were nevertheless the first big success of what became known as 'The Showband Era'. The band was founded back in the 1940s by Hugh Tourish and became 'The Clipper Carlton' in 1949. They acquired a new manager, Victor Craig and after some personnel changes, the lineup was Hugo Quinn on trumpet, Victor Fleming on trombone, Hugh Tourish on piano, Terry Logue on sax and clarinet, Mick O'Hanlon on drums, Art O'Hagan on string bass and singer Fergus O'Hanlon. Like many innovators, The Clipper Carlton may have been just a little bit ahead of their time. They were certainly the first big showband in the country but in the early Sixties they became eclipsed by a new generation of showbands which had a new ingredient – the featured singer.

And the first and greatest of those was Brendan Bowyer.

My first real encounter with showbands was when we went along to see Brendan Bowyer and the Royal Showband in Galway. I was over there with Earl Gill and we had heard how this young band from Waterford was packing large ballrooms to capacity and generating near hysteria among the dancers. When we walked into the ballroom, we understood why. The Royal had developed a distinctive sound in which electric guitars and brass were strongly featured and in Brendan Bowyer they had a great star. Son of Stanley Bowyer, a distinguished organist and classical musician, young Brendan was a talented boy soprano and then sang and played trombone in local bands including The Rhythm Kings before going to work in the office of a Waterford paper mill. He was recruited by sax player Michael Coppinger and guitarist Jim Conlan, who were then playing with The Harry Boland Band but were planning to form a new showband along the lines of The Clipper Carlton. They had already signed up Charlie Matthews (drums), Tom Dunphy (guitar and vocals) and Gerry Cullen (keyboards) and would later add Eddie Sullivan (trumpet) to the lineup. Some of the band members had bought their instruments on hire-purchase from a mail-order company called Cotts of Kilcock and had become friendly with a salesman called T. J. Byrne. He took a keen interest in the new band and had become their manager when they were launched in October 1957, with a name inspired by the local Theatre Royal.

The Royal Showband were an instant phenomenon and, on that night in Galway, I understood why. They looked well in their blazers and slacks, moved around the stage, swaying to the music, played all the current hit songs and had hugely entertaining singers. Tom Dunphy did the country songs, which were then very popular, while Brendan Bowyer specialised in rock numbers including his own unique 'take' on Elvis Presley. He could also belt out the big ballads and had his own showstoppers like *The Croppy Boy* and *The Holy City* – the song I had performed all those years ago in my audition for Molly Coulihan's Stage School in Crumlin.

The Royal were to have an outstanding career of course. They were the first Irish showband to make a record, they had several No. 1 hits in this country, they were the first showband to tour America and, in 1961, they won the Carl Allen Award in Britain having been chosen as 'Most Outstanding Modern Dance Band of the Year'. In later years Brendan Bowyer went to live in Las

Vegas and was a star attraction on The Strip for more than two decades. His audience even included Elvis Presley who would slip across the road from Caesars Palace to the Stardust to catch Brendan's act. Indeed I have the same Brendan to thank for my one and only appearance in Las Vegas. I was on holiday with Sheila and my daughter Aisling and we went to see his show. He spotted me in the audience and kindly invited me up on stage to sing a song or two. So I was able to add Vegas to the list of places where I had entertained. Thank you Brendan; you are a real gentleman and it is great to hear you singing as well as ever today.

When Earl Gill and the other members of our band watched The Royal Showband, we quickly realised that a new era in Irish dance music was born and that we would have to change if we were to survive. In the months that followed, it seemed that a new showband was being launched every week and most of them had featured singers, including a small number who are still in the business today. The first big showband to come out of Dublin was The Capitol, which was formed as a semi-professional group in 1959 and went fully professional a few years later. This was a common pattern among the showbands as many of their members were still either studying or had jobs which they did not want to quit in favour of an uncertain career in showbusiness. The Royal, for instance, were two years on the road before they became a professional band and in the case of The Capitol, a few of their members were still at university. Such was the case of Des Kelly from Galway who played in local bands with his brother Johnny before moving to Dublin to study at UCD, where he became friendly with trumpet player Paul Sweeney and pianist Eamon Monaghan. They began gigging around Dublin and were spotted by Tom Doherty who suggested that they form a showband. They recruited a few musicians from other bands including Jimmy Hogan from The Blue Clavons, Don Long on trombone who had been playing with Donie Collins in Limerick, Paddy Cole from Castleblayney on sax who had been with The Maurice Lynch Band and James 'Butch' Moore, a printing apprentice who was then singing with Billy Carter in the National Ballroom.

The Capitol Showband was launched in 1961 with Tom Doherty's brother Jim as manager and they went on to achieve great success over the next decade or so. Butch became the first Irish representative in the Eurovision Song Contest when he sang *Walking the Streets in the Rain* in 1965 and was placed sixth. He was the first in a succession of showband singers who would represent Ireland at Eurovision in the following years. Dickie Rock, who had shot to fame with The Miami Showband, was placed fourth with Roland Soper's song *Come Back to Stay*, in 1966 and Sean Dunphy was runner up to Sandy Shaw the following year with *If I Could Choose*, a song co-written by Wesley Burrows who was the principal writer of RTÉ series like *The Riordans* and *Glenroe*. Our representative in 1968 was Pat McGeegan who sang John Kennedy's song *Chance of a Lifetime*. Pat was then lead singer with The Big Four and we were to become great friends in later years when we frequently met on the road. He is of course also the father of world champion boxer Barry McGuigan. Muriel Day and the Lindsays were placed seventh in 1969 with *The Wages of Love* before Dana became our first Eurovision winner in 1970 with *All Kinds of Everything*.

I mention these successes to illustrate the high quality of the showband singers as musicians and entertainers. They have often been dismissed as mere copyists but in fact the showband era developed a whole generation of talented musicians who had wonderful 'ears' and could create all the sounds of the day, as well as competing on the international stage.

The Capitol Showband, for instance, went on to play to a television audience of 30 million viewers on *Sunday Night at the London Palladium* and also appeared on UK TV shows like *Thank Your Lucky Stars* and The *Eamon Andrews Show*. Butch Moore eventually moved to The Kings Showband and later developed a successful career on the cabaret circuit in the USA. Barry Cluskey, who was leader of The Kings, later teamed up with Des Hopkins, son of dance band leader Jimmy Hopkins, to form The Cluskey Hopkins Jazz Band, which still plays at festivals in many parts of Europe.

In the early Sixties, showbands began to emerge in every city and town of Ireland. Most were semi-professional outfits but the number of professional bands began to grow rapidly. Cork had The Dixielanders who included Brendan O'Brien and the legendary Joe Mac who was a blend of drummer, singer, comedian and all-round entertainer. We became good friends in later years and we still meet up every October Bank Holiday to play at the Fringe Jazz Festival in Kinsale – but more of that later. Having started it all with The Royal Showband, Waterford then produced The Blue Aces, while Limerick had Tommy Drennan and the Monarchs, Cavan had Larry Cunningham and the Mighty Avons, Kilkenny had The Black Aces, and Mullingar produced one of Ireland's greatest-ever entertainers, Joe Dolan and his band The Drifters.

Earl Gill's band continued to do fairly well in this new environment. We changed the programme and included a *South Pacific* show during which we would pump dry ice onto the stage for effect. It was inevitable that I would eventually become part of the showband scene. It fact it was necessary for survival because that was where the work now existed. My chance came when I was approached by Mick Quinn and Robert McGrattan who were in the process of forming a new professional showband out of the semi-pro Royal Olympics. They recruited trumpeter Freddie Martin from the Neil Kearns Orchestra, Sean Fagan as a vocalist and myself from The Earl Gill Band. We began to rehearse in the Mayfair Ballroom in Clondalkin in preparation for our launch as The Pacific Showband in Romano's Ballroom, Belfast on Easter Saturday 1961. This was a new form of rehearsal for me as up until then I would play from sheet music either bought from Waltons or May's or written out by Earl or Jim Farley. With The Pacific, as in other showbands, the arrangements were compiled from listening to records. The bands needed to include the hits in their programme well before sheet music scores would become available and so we would buy records of all the latest hits and each band member would listen carefully to his particular part and reproduce it as accurately as possible. The rhythm section, for instance, would study the chord changes and learn their part and the brass would then add their contribution while the singers learned the tune, the words, the phrasing and even the accent. We would actually write out the lyrics *from* the record, going over it again and again and then learn the melody. In order to work in this environment, you needed to be both a good musician and have a very good 'ear'. Sean Fagan had a brilliant ear and would pick up an entire arrangement, getting it right first time. We spent long Tuesdays in Clondalkin and would consider it a good day's work if we perfected three or four numbers. When the band was launched, we were on the road five nights a week and also spent one of our free days in rehearsal. The dancers expected to hear all the hits featured on *The Top 20* or *Ireland's Top 10,* which meant that the life span of a number in our set list was only a few weeks and each week we had to rehearse new material. It was a long shot from the swing orchestras where standards like *In the Mood* could be on the set list for a decade or more. Once again I was fortunate to work with some very talented musicians in The Pacific. They included Freddie Martin on trumpet, Harry Parker on bass, Shay Curran on keyboards, Marty Fanning on drums, Jimmy Dumpleton on guitar and Sean Fagan on trombone and vocals. Although I was the tenor sax player in the band (I waved it around a lot), I was hired primarily as a singer and I specialised in tunes by Perry Como, Frank Sinatra and Matt Munro while Sean specialised in the big ballads of Roy Orbison.

Not only showbands were multiplying in those first years of the Sixties – so were the ballrooms in which they played. All over the country, local businessmen and promoters were building large, and occasionally enormous, ballrooms which were attracting thousands of dancers every night of the week. Dublin had its traditional ballrooms of course like the National, Olympic, Crystal and Ballerina but new venues also emerged including the Country Club in Portmarnock and Laurel Park in Bray. Around the country there were 'prestige venues' like the Arcadia in Cork, the Stella in Limerick, the Ambassador in Ballybunion, the Astoria in Bundoran, the Hangar and Seapoint in Galway. These were supplemented by literally hundreds of new venues such as the Oyster Ballroom in Dromkeen, Co. Limerick built by local merchant Paddy Hayes literally at a crossroads. Typical of these venues, the Oyster was a concrete structure with a large sprung maple dance floor, an upstairs balcony featuring a mineral bar, ladies' and gents' cloakrooms and toilets and little else apart from a large car park. Facilities for the bands were minimal; a chilly room in which to get changed was all many offered. Yet they attracted thousands of dancers from a catchment area of up to 60 miles. As well as the top showbands of the day, the Oyster hosted international acts like Jim Reeves, Hank Locklin, The Bachelors and even the Johnny Dankworth Orchestra with Cleo Laine. When the great clarinet player Sid Phillips played there in the early Sixties, he and his fellow musicians camped out for the night in a nearby field.

The 'Ballroom Kings' of the Sixties, of course, were former Taoiseach Albert Reynolds and his brother Jim. They built a chain of ballrooms located strategically around the country, each of which incorporated the word 'Land' in the name. You could spend the entire year just touring the Reynolds ballrooms and to get on their list was a guarantee of dates, large attendances and success. During my days with The Pacific, we spent a lot of our time playing in venues like the Borderland in Clones, Cloudland in Rooskey, Danceland in Portlaoise, Dreamland in Athy, Fairyland in Roscommon, Barrowland in New Ross and Jetland in Limerick, where we played our very first gig. The Reynolds ballrooms were of a higher standard than many in the country at the time and the facilities for musicians were generally better.

Over those years we got to know every corner of Ireland as we traversed the country in our bandwagon. This was one of our luxuries – a Mercedes coach which was custom-built by a company from Dundalk. It had very comfortable aircraft style seats and was air conditioned. Depending on where we were playing that night, we would all meet up in Dublin around mid-day and set off for our destination which could be in Kerry or

Donegal. The lads would chat for a while and then maybe play cards or tell yarns but in truth I rarely participated. I could 'sleep for Ireland' in those days and no sooner would we reach the Naas Dual Carriageway than I would have nodded off, not to awake until we stopped somewhere for a meal. It was the same on the long journey home after the dance – I would also be the first asleep. Dances generally ran from 9pm to 1am and occasionally 2am and, as The Pacific became more popular, we could arrange for a relief band to play the first hour or so. Nevertheless once we went on stage, we were playing flat out for several hours, with maybe just one short interval. We were on our feet all the time and did a little bit of dancing or swaying to the beat and of course the brass players waved their instruments about. You would be pretty well whacked at the end of the night. It did not end there either because the gear had to be taken down and packed into the bus. We might be lucky enough to get a cup of tea and a ham sandwich before we hit the road back to Dublin. This was the case with most of the bands who would end the night pretty hungry, so we would tend to stop on the way home at a few restaurants or chippers that would be open at that hour. Places like Dirty Dicks in Thomondgate, Limerick or Wongs on the Naas Road were great places to meet the other bands. We would all be having steaks and chips and a few drinks and would exchange stories of who was playing where, what bands were being formed or breaking up and who was attracting big crowds. Some showband musicians were heavy drinkers and sadly some had serious problems with alcohol during their careers. Although I enjoyed a drink, I was never a very serious drinker but I always enjoyed meeting a few special friends on the road for a few scoops. My good friends at that time included Pat McGeegan whom I have already mentioned and Davy McKnight who was drummer with Billy Brown and the Freshmen. This Belfast band specialised in close harmony singing with very accurate covers of The Beach Boys and Davy was the high note singer. Other members of The Freshmen included Barney McKeon (vocals), Maurice Henry (sax), Torry McGahey (bass), Damian McIlroy (guitar) and Sean Mahon (trombone), while Tommy Drennan, later of The Monarchs, was also a member for a few years.

Being cooped up in a coach for long hours, five days a week, naturally created some tensions. A stray remark or maybe an incident on the previous night or a band member turning up late and delaying departure could all result in a bit of narkiness. We would come across stories of bands not talking to each other for days on end but I must say that in The Pacific we all got on fairly well with each other.

There was a lot of good natured banter and joking on the road and bands would write messages to each other (which were not always polite) on dressing room mirrors. My own 'mirror memory' concerns such a dressing room in which the ballroom owner had thoughtfully provided small individual mirrors so that the bands could check their appearance before going on stage. I thought that this would be a worthwhile addition to my kit-bag and so I slipped Sean Fagan's mirror into my pocket. Later in the coach, I admitted to Sean that I had stolen his mirror. 'Don't worry, Sonny,' he replied, 'I nicked yours.'

For me, the biggest drawback of being in a showband was the huge amount of time I spent away from Sheila and my young family. Looking back on those days, I realise that Geraldine and Gary grew up behind my back and I missed many of those golden moments which parents are privileged to experience with their young children. Indeed it was left to Sheila to do the many things that parents share in the rearing of their children. She enrolled them in the local schools and drove them there and back every day. Both Geraldine and Gary would say that the reason their Mammy drove a car was because Daddy was always away and she had to learn so that they could get to school. It was the same with parent-teacher meetings and other school events such as sports days or concerts. Always it was Sheila who went along to these and it was I who missed out because I was on a ballroom stage somewhere around the country. On Geraldine's First Holy Communion Day, I was in Belfast and the band would not give me the night off so I had to drive down to Dublin, attend the Mass and then drive back to Belfast for the gig. That was the downside of being in a showband.

I was tempted into showband life by the promise of good money and I suppose the fear that the big dance bands would not be around for very long. Overall it was probably a disappointing experience, for while I was well paid, The Pacific was not owned by the musicians who were paid a weekly wage, unlike some of the other showbands such as The Royal, The Clipper Carlton and The Royal Blues, which were co-ops in which all members shared equally.

Singing and playing with The Pacific was however rewarding and enjoyable from a professional point of view. I got to expand my repertoire enormously singing the hit songs of Matt Munro, Perry Como, Andy Williams, Tony Bennett and others while Sean became Ireland's version of Roy Orbison. Other band members also sang, with Marty Fanning contributing Jim Reeves songs. Every Lent, when dancing came to a standstill in Ireland (such was the influence of the Catholic Bishops), we went off to tour the Irish clubs in Britain and met many other showbands who were on the same circuit. Indeed, it was on one of these tours that I first struck up a friendship with Pat McGeegan. We also did just one tour of America, a good ten years after I had toured there with Ruby Murray.

The showband era also gave me my first recording opportunities. Until then I had made just one record and it was 'as Gaeilge'. It was part of a project initiated by Gael Linn to make Irish popular among teenagers. The songs on the record were *Mi Iomlain* and *An Bfhuil an Fonn Sinn Ort?* and the musicians included the late great jazz drummer John Wadham and jazz pianist Ian Henry, neither of whom were exactly 'Gaeilgeoirí'.

That was the extent of my recording career until the time came when getting a record into the Irish Top 20 became a marketing necessity for the showbands. The Royal Showband had started the trend with an unlikely hit called *Come Down the Mountain Katy Daly* and they were followed by The Capitol who had a hit with *Foolin' Time* written by a young Phil Coulter. Then Dickie Rock burst on the scene with The Miami Showband and he had a big first No. 1 in 1963 with *There's Always Me*. If The Pacific were to stay in the top league of showbands, we needed hit records also and so we went into the recording studios for the first time in 1964. Sean Fagan was the featured singer on our first single, which was called *She Wears My Ring* with *Stand Beside Me* on the B side. It was an immediate hit and went straight to No. 1 Sean followed this with another hit cover version of Roy Orbison's *Distant Drums* with *Photograph to the Wall* on the B side.

Our next recording was what might be described as 'outside the box'. We were approached by Tommy Ellis, who had a recording studio in Dublin, to see if we would support a charity record which would feature Sr. Mary Gertrude, the 'Irish Singing

Nun'. We agreed because it was a good cause and the record would certainly generate valuable publicity so we drove out to Ardmore Film Studios in Bray for the session. Sr. Mary Gertrude, who was a lovely lady and a very nice singer, laid down her track called *Evening in Mellary* and then Sean and I shared the vocals on a tune called *My Auld Killarney Hat*. Needless to say it was a big hit and a copy found its way into every convent in Ireland.

My own first record with The Pacific was cut in 1965. The song was called *No One Will Ever Know* and a B side called *If You Knew*. It sold well and reached No. 3 or 4 in the charts and I followed it up the following year with *No One Knows*, which made me wonder if I really knew anything at all! The B side of that record was a little known gem called *The Menace from Ennis,* which was one of the songs in the National Song Contest that year – another piece of trivia which may be of use some day in a pub quiz.

Mick Quinn decided that it would be a good idea if both of The Pacific singers featured on a single record and so Sean Fagan and I combined in 1966 to record a duet called *I Only Came to Dance with You,* which had some nice harmony singing as did the B side called *Sleepless Nights*. That particular recording was made in London and our backing singers included Con and Dec Cluskey of The Bachelors, who were then a huge act in Britain. From then onwards, over the next few years, Sean and I alternated as lead singer on Pacific Showband recordings, which until 1967, were on the Pye label and, from then until 1970, were on Tribune. The year 1965 was particularly prolific from this point of view. Sean recorded *What's the Use?* and *Do What I Want You To* and later I made *We Could* with the Pat Boone song *When the Swallows Come Back to Capistrano* with Sean rounding off the year with *This Time* and *Just to Satisfy You*. I kicked off 1966 with that rousing old ballad *The Dublin Fusiliers* backed by *Edelweiss* from *The Sound of Music* and Sean followed with *For He's a Jolly Good Fellow,* which was coupled with *She Thinks I Still Care. My Jenny* and *Since I Don't Have You* followed and finally in 1968, *My Lovely Rose and You* (a song that remains in my repertoire) and *I'll Remember You,* which is perhaps better known from the instrumental version by Benny Goodman.

Recording in those days was a relatively straightforward affair. The bands selected their songs and wrote out arrangements (or hired arrangers to do the job). They then booked a studio and hired session musicians who rehearsed the arrangement, sometimes with the singer and sometimes on their own. If backing singers were involved, they would also lay down their tracks. (I was a backing singer on many of these sessions, but you won't find me in the credits.) Once a 'clean take' of the backing was in place, the session musicians would pack up and go away. The singer would then come into the studio to record the vocal track and an engineer would mix it all together. I don't remember 'record producers' such as we have today – just an engineer or maybe two at a sound desk who would stop things if a mistake occurred and who would play over each 'take' until everybody was satisfied. We had some great session musicians including Johnny Tate, John Curran and Johnny Christopher, as well as Joe McIntyre who was from Northern Ireland and was one of the greatest trumpet players of that era. He was from a musical family and was a cousin of Gay McIntyre who had his own band for many years. The tradition continues through the latest generation – Joey McIntyre who plays on the Dublin scene. I enjoyed recording as I had a good memory for lyrics and had a lot of experience singing with band arrangements. As a result

I would generally get it right first time around and I became known in the business as 'One Take Sonny'. We both had successful recording careers, with Sean making the No. 1 spot on three occasions while my singles tended to make No. 3 or 4.

Having a hit record was highly important from an image point of view and also in getting airplays on Radio Éireann or even Radio Caroline. It also helped a band get a spot on radio programmes like *The 17 Club* or even *The Showband Show* on RTÉ television. This weekly show hosted by Paul Russell was the Irish equivalent of *Top of the Pops* and an appearance would help boost pulling power and the fees or door percentage which a band could demand. Managers therefore used every strategy they could dream up to boost record sales. We handed out free singles at dances, and radio presenters and producers of sponsored programmes were lobbied incessantly to play particular records. There was much talk of bribery and corruption but I never encountered anything of that ilk for the good reason that my entire life was spent travelling to dances or rehearsing. I did however make my first TV appearance with The Pacific on *The Showband Show* and my records tended to be favourites with presenters like Gay Byrne and Val Joyce.

The showband era had begun in the late Fifties and by the closing years of the Sixties, the phenomenon was on the wane. Bands were splitting up or forming new combinations, attendances in the ballrooms were falling and some venues were closing up shop. The first major breakup occurred when Tommy Swarbrigg left Joe Dolan and the Drifters to form The Times. Soon afterwards Joe Mac and Brendan O'Brien left The Dixies to form Stage 2, while several members of The Miami left to form The Sands. Of course The Royal Showband had split into two, with The Big Eight featuring Brendan Bowyer and Tom Dunphy and augmented by Paddy Cole from The Capitol moving for most of the year to The Stardust in Las Vegas. Meanwhile two new breeds of band emerged – country music outfits like The Cotton Mill Boys and The Smokey Mountain Ramblers and pop bands like The Memories and Chips.

It was not difficult to see the writing on the wall for the showbands and The Pacific decided to take a pragmatic approach by emigrating lock, stock and barrel to Canada where they were to be known as Dublin Corporation. I was mulling over whether I would emigrate with the band when the problem was solved for me in an unexpected manner. Des Smith called around one evening and said, 'Sonny – do you have any whiskey?'

'I don't,' I replied.

'Well,' he said, 'make a cup of tea because you are going to need it.'

Over the cuppa, Des explained that he had heard from 'reliable sources' that I was going to be dropped from The Pacific because I was considered to be too old and not photogenic enough. Needless to say, I was flabbergasted but when I cooled down I realised that it might all be for the best. After all I was married with two young children and it did not suit me at all to emigrate as neither Sheila nor I had any ambition to live outside of Dublin. We talked it over and as my contract with The Pacific had almost expired, I decided to take preemptive action and resign before they could fire me. It was the best decision of my career. Very shortly afterwards I was approached by Dermot O'Brien, then leader of The Clubmen, who offered me a place in his band. I had been recommended to him by George O'Reilly who knew that I had decided against going to Canada. I accepted happily but I had to be replaced by two people in The Pacific. Peter Law came into the band as vocalist while Paddy ('Podger') Reynolds joined on sax. The band did well in Canada as Dublin Corporation and I still have regular contact with Sean Fagan who now lives in Toronto.

At one stage Dermot O'Brien, who hailed from Ardee, was better known as a sportsman than a musician. A talented athlete and Gaelic footballer, he had captained Louth to a rare All Ireland victory in 1957 and was very proud of his All Ireland medal, which his wife Rosemary had made into a brooch. He was also a very talented accordionist and a singer who was blessed with an ability to always sing perfectly in tune. Being an excellent musician himself, Dermot had surrounded himself with like-minded people. The band included Donal O'Dowda, a nephew of the Percy French specialist Brendan O'Dowda. Sadly Donal died in a car accident some years later. Other members included Frank 'Bunk' Darcy on drums (he got his nickname because he was a big fan of the Dixieland 'great', Bunk Johnson) and Benny Kindillon on guitar, a musician who still plays with me on the cabaret scene today and who has been a great friend and supporter over the years.

The band played a mixture of Irish, country and pop music and I contributed my Matt Munro and similar numbers. We appeared on television in the *Maisie McDaniel Show* and at the Royal Albert Hall in London on an Irish special night that also featured The Johnsons folk group (which included Paul Brady) and The Dubliners. The Royal Albert Hall holds 8,000 people and is an enormous auditorium. Dermot, who was well used to playing to large audiences, took the gig in his stride but I was very nervous. My condition was hardly helped by the late Ronnie Drew who took me on a walk through a very long circular corridor of dressing rooms. On reaching one room, Ronnie opened the door to reveal Luke Kelly, stretched out on a table, deep in alcohol-induced sleep. 'Look at that,' said Ronnie, 'Isn't stage fright a terrible thing?'

My own stage fright took an upward leap after that but although walking on stage was a daunting experience, once we got going I felt fine and the gig was a great success.

My period with Dermot O'Brien was brief – a mere two years at the end of the showband era. We both knew that 'The Times – They are A-Changin'', to quote Bob Dylan, and that we would have to once again find a new direction if we were to survive as professional musicians.

What that direction would be remained uncertain. But as the big ballrooms sold out to the supermarkets, the final bottles of minerals were consumed and the 'Hucklebuck' became just one more dance novelty from the past, a door opened which let me enter a musical world in which I have lived ever since.

Welcome to Cabaret.

CHAPTER **7**

Come to the
Cabaret

With the decline of the showbands, popular music in
Ireland spread out in several directions. Teenagers had
abandoned jiving for the music of The Beatles and other groups,
most of whom were from Liverpool. 'Merseybeat' was the
current craze and from the mid Sixties onwards, showbands
were including Beatles hits in their sets along with the numbers
recorded by groups like Gerry and the Pacemakers, The
Searchers, The Swinging Blue Jeans, Billy J. Kramer, Freddie and
the Dreamers, Herman's Hermits, The Hollies, Brian Poole and
the Tremeloes, and The Dave Clarke Five. Many of these groups
toured the Irish ballrooms but they did not always play to 'full
houses'. The beat groups had guitar-based lineups with no brass

or reed players and as a result their music was at odds with the showband sound. It did not take too long for young Irish beat groups to emerge and they tended to play in small clubs, along the lines of Liverpool's famous Cavern Club, which began to pop up in Dublin, Cork, Limerick and other cities and towns. Suddenly an alternative circuit to the Reynolds ballrooms began to emerge. Danny Hughes, a good friend of mine over many years, was among the pioneers of this club scene as was John Ryan who ran a very successful club in the centre of Dublin. Towards the mid Sixties the Merseybeat began to give way to a more strident form of rock pioneered by bands like The Who, The Rolling Stones and the Irish group Them whose lead singer was one Van Morrison. The group enjoyed huge success on its first tour of the USA with hits like *Gloria* which remains a Van the Man favourite today. A band called Horslips created their own spin on current trends by merging traditional Irish dance tunes with beat rhythms but the really successful Irish acts of that genre spent most of their time outside of this country, touring in Britain and America. They included Rory Gallagher who was born in Ballyshannon but grew up in Cork. A musical prodigy, he played guitar from the age of 12 when he won a local talent contest and actually began his professional career with The Fontana Showband. The Stratocaster guitar, which he bought in 1961 and which stayed with him throughout his career, also has a showband link as it was once owned by Jim Conlon of The Royal Showband. Rory, who passed away in 1995, became one of the greatest blues guitarists of all time whose memory is still revered whenever and wherever the blues are played.

Skid Row were a hugely popular group among young Dubliners in the early Seventies but it was Thin Lizzie, with the iconic Phil Lynott, which became the first Irish rock group to make it big in Britain while remaining based here in Ireland. They had a huge hit with *Whiskey in the Jar*, played on *Top of the Pops* with the likes of Stevie Wonder and were a most exciting live act when they took the stage. They were also an inspiration for a new generation of Irish rock bands who rehearsed in garages and played in the small clubs where the teenagers of the early Seventies liked to hang out. Many of these young musicians liked to play music, which they had composed individually or on a co-operative basis with other band members, and this was perhaps their most significant contribution to the development of popular music in this country.

The beat clubs, which tended to be small, dark and very noisy, did not of course appeal to everyone. A slightly older generation flocked to the new nightclubs, which also began to appear in the cities. Zhivago in Dublin's Baggot Street was marketed with the slogan 'Where Love Stories Begin' and was highly popular. These clubs were hosts to bands like Bagatelle, The Greenbeats, Chips and Stepaside, which could also be heard in venues like The Baggot Inn. In parallel with these large clubs came the emergence of nightclubs which were concentrated in an area of Leeson Street dubbed 'The Strip' after its more famous namesake in Las Vegas. These clubs with names like 'The Pink Elephant' and 'Elizabeth's' played disco music into the early morning hours and traded technically as restaurants with wine licences. Around the same time, hotels around the country discovered a loophole in the law which enabled them to apply for late night bar extensions on the basis of a 'special occasion'. The Courts found difficulty in defining what a 'special occasion' meant and the result was that exemptions could be obtained for any night of the week except Saturday. This development facilitated an extended evening of entertainment, which would typically include a set by a live band followed by a disco.

However the most significant development of all on the entertainment scene was not music–related. It was more about liberated Irish women in the Sixties going into bars for a drink. During the showband era, the normal sequence of events on a dance night was for the men to have a few pints in the local pub before they went to the ballroom, while the ladies tended to go directly to the dance. Ballrooms did not have a licence to sell alcohol and refreshments were confined to soft drinks. On a good night, a ballroom could sell several thousand bottles of Club Orange or Lucozade. At some point during the Sixties, the ladies also took to going to the pub and publicans began to think of ways of keeping them there rather than see everyone trotting off to the dance around 10pm. They began to provide entertainment – and the pub cabaret scene was born.

The first pub entertainers were the pub customers themselves. The publican hired a musician who was also a Master of Ceremonies and he invited customers to come up to the mike and do their party pieces. These 'singing pubs' became a popular feature of the Dublin scene. They attracted a more mature audience, usually married couples of all ages who cheered each other's efforts and sang along to choruses of mainly Irish songs. Many of our best known entertainers, including Colm Wilkinson, learned their trade in these venues. This form of entertainment, which has its origins in house parties and 'hooleys' has proven to be enduring and has survived a whole series of trends from discos to karaoke. You will still find people gathering in pubs all over the country for a sing-along led by a local musician who knows what everybody sings, what key they sing in and when they are likely to forget the words. Sheila and

I really enjoy an evening in a 'singing pub' and you will often find us on a Saturday night during the Summer in Hamill's pub in Kilmuckridge where we have a holiday home. Singers are invited to sing just one number – that's the house rule – but I have got around this once or twice by doing one of my medleys. Mention of the 'singing pubs' reminds me of an incident involving Sheila's mother who was a real 'home bird' and seldom went out to social events. Some time after the death of her husband, she was persuaded by the family to go along to a musical session in a pub. Reluctantly she agreed and really enjoyed the evening. The crowd hung around well after closing time and eventually the Gardaí arrived to clear the house. They started taking names of all those present, including Sheila's mother who had never been to a pub before in her life, and on her very first visit at more than 70 years of age, almost got herself arrested.

Outside of Dublin, the early cabaret acts were principally folk groups. The Dubliners, The Wolfe Tones, The Johnstons, The Ludlow Trio and The Dublin City Ramblers packed out the cabaret rooms which were being added to pubs around the country. Christy Moore also emerged on this circuit as did The Pecker Dunne, Danny Doyle and Johnny McEvoy. Suddenly folk music was replacing rock in terms of radio airtime. It seems unbelievable now but people would happily drive up to 60 miles to a pub for an evening of drinking and cabaret.

My first introduction to the cabaret scene came after I had decided to leave Dermot O'Brien who was himself going off in a new direction and later moved to live in Florida. I was asked to sing a few songs and be MC in Biddy Mulligan's, a pub in The Coombe, which ran a very popular cabaret featuring people like Joe Cahill and Hal Roach. This was another new experience for me as I was there with no band and no rehearsal. I would just ask the lads in the house band to follow me – and they usually did so with great skill. By now many of the former showband musicians had begun to turn up on the cabaret circuit and they were experts at impromptu playing and devising arrangements. They are brilliant musicians who only need to get a hint of a tune, or a few chords, to provide a high class backing. They have been there throughout my entire career in cabaret and I owe them a great debt of gratitude for accompanying me, frequently without any rehearsal, over many years.

The Biddy Mulligan's gig led to another in Slattery's of Terenure, which has been a famous pub over the years and a centre of activity for the local community. Pat O'Donnell, who ran the cabaret there, invited me to MC the show once a week and this led to another regular Friday spot at the Molly Malone pub in Little Green Street, just around the corner from the Special Criminal Court where many high profile trials have taken place in recent times. Eddie Finlay was the band leader there and we developed a system of signalling to each other which I have retained ever since. Two fingers upwards (no – NOT a 'Harvey Smith') meant the key was sharp and the same two fingers pointing down indicated a move to flat. Shortly afterwards I added another show to my weekly schedule at the Clare Manor in Raheny.

In order to cope with this rapidly growing career in pub cabaret, I had to extend my repertoire and develop a patter for my MC role. On the musical side I looked to my singing heroes like Matt Monro and Max Bygraves whom – I have no hesitation in admitting – I 'robbed blind' in terms of copying their songs. I also started singing medleys of tunes which fitted easily together, a formula I first tried out in the Earl Gill Band.

'Why do one song when you can get away with five' was Earl's advice. So I put together medleys of tunes like *Moonlight and Roses, Roses are Shining in Picardy* and *I'm Gonna Sit Right Down and Write Myself a Letter*, which are still in my sets today. Most of these songs are classics which older people love to sing and which today's generation remember from hearing them sung by their parents or grandparents.

It was around this time too that I became conscious of my trademark 'wave' to the audience while I am singing. Tommy Orr, who was MC at Molly Malone's introduced me to the audience one evening by saying, 'Here he is ... the Window Cleaner Himself ... Sonny Knowles.' I went on and did my act and afterwards I asked Tommy what all this 'window washer thing' was about.

'Don't you know, Sonny?' he said, 'When you sing you wave to the audience as if you were washing windows.'

'No, I don't,' I replied. 'I never do that.'

'Well – watch out for it next time you sing.' he said.

So on my next date at Molly's, I decided to be conscious of my hand movements – and lo and behold – I saw myself doing the 'window washing' routine. I was delighted of course because it was a distinctive way of communicating with the audience and they responded very well. So I decided to make it part of my act and to even 'ham it up' on occasions. The result was magic. From then onwards I would 'window wash' at the audience and they would 'window wash' back to me. When I did shows in America years later, the audience would start to wave at me even before I sang a note. So I am proud to be 'The Window Washer' and today the audiences and I have a great time waving to each other during my act. Even truck drivers give me the 'window wash' if they see me driving by.

As the pub cabaret scene in Dublin developed, newer and larger venues emerged, such as the Braemor Room in Churchtown, the Old Sheiling in Raheny and the Tudor Room off Parnell Square. One of the most successful was the Drake Inn in Finglas, one of two pubs owned by the McKiernan family. Billy Hughes, who was MC and entertainer there, was working every night of the week and needed to get two nights off. He introduced me to Pat McKiernan who hadn't a clue who I was but nevertheless gave me the job for two nights a week – Tuesdays and Thursdays. This was a major breakthrough for me at the time because the Drake Inn was not only one of the biggest and most popular cabaret venues in Dublin but it also hosted a big name Guest Star every week. I would usually open the show with a 45-minute set and then introduce the star attraction who might be Frank Ifield, Matt Monro, Kathy Kirby, Harry Secombe, magician Paul Daniels or the comedienne Marti Caine. These entertainers were at the top of their profession in Britain and watching them work was a most educational experience. The singers would usually come over with their musical director and would forward copies of their music a week in advance together with the lineup of musicians they required. Because of my background playing with dance bands and the RTÉ orchestras, I had many contacts among musicians. As a result I landed the job of putting the backing bands together and going through the initial rehearsals. The big acts were usually booked for a week-long run and on the day before the opening show, the musical director would take control of the rehearsal so that the singer could just walk on stage and get into the act as if he or she were at the 'Talk of the Town' in London.

Frank Ifield was a very big star at the time and a regular on the London Palladium. When he toured Britain in 1963, his support act was The Beatles. Frank had four No. 1 hits in a single year, including *I Remember You* which sold more than a million copies, *Lovesick Blues, Wayward Wind* and *Confession.* He represented Britain twice in the Eurovision Song Contest with *Alone Too Long* which was runner-up in 1962 and *Ain't Going to Take no for an Answer* which was 12th (and last) in 1976. He was still going strong in 1991 when a comeback record of *She Taught Me to Yodel,* a song popular with the Royal Showband, made the charts. When he sang at the Drake Inn, I told him that I had covered his record *Three Good Reasons* and to watch out for an audience reaction when he sang the song. 'When you sing about "One" they will all raise one finger. When you sing "Two" you will get two fingers – but don't worry, they are just counting along with you,' I warned.

And of course that's what happened.

Frank and I got on famously when he was here and I had the great pleasure of catching up with him again many years later in Australia.

Harry Secombe was a larger-than-life character in every respect and a great ambassador for his native Wales. He first met up with Spike Milligan when they were both in the British Army fighting in Tunisia during World War II and afterwards they starred in the hilarious BBC radio show *The Goons* in which Harry played the role of *Neddie Seagoon.* He also had a regular role in *Educating Archie,* another BBC radio comedy series. Harry was a rare mixture of comedian, actor and singer. He had a wonderful voice which was trained by the Italian maestro Manlio di Veroli and once did a routine in which he sang both the baritone and falsetto parts in the duet *Sweethearts.* He was in the lead role in the 1963 film *Pickwick,* a musical based on the Charles Dickens novel *The Pickwick Papers,* during which he sang *If I Ruled the World* which was his first major hit. He followed this in 1967 with *This is My Song* and later he was truly magnificent as *Mr. Bumble* in the film version of *Oliver!.*

When he appeared for a week at the Drake Inn in the early 1970s, Harry was at the height of his powers and was a huge attraction. I was the MC for the show and I had also put the backing band together. Rehearsals went well and on the afternoon of the opening night, I got a request to visit Harry in his dressing room. I went along thinking that he had specific instructions about how he should be introduced, as was the practice with other stars of the day. When I opened the door, I was greeted by this enormous man with a great big smile and a warm handshake.

'Delighted to meet you, Sonny,' he said, 'What will you have to drink?'

'Well – what do you have?' I enquired.

'Just about everything. Pat McKiernan has given me a full bar for the week.'

'In that case, I'll have a ball of malt.'

We sat there chatting in the most relaxed way over a few glasses of whiskey, until eventually I thought I should get down to the business in hand.

'What do you want me to say this evening when you are being introduced?' I asked.

'Whatever comes into your head – you're the man in charge,' he replied with a big laugh.

'But I thought you invited me up here to give me instructions.'

'Not at all, Sonny,' he said – and the laugh got bigger and louder. 'I just wanted to meet you and have a drink with you before the show.'

Of course, there was no need to say anything before Harry took the stage. The crowd was buzzing with anticipation and as soon as I announced his name, there was huge applause. He did not disappoint his audience, presenting a marvellous show which included jokes, anecdotes, mimicry and that wonderful voice.

In the 1980s and 1990s, Harry was best known as a presenter of the religious programme *Songs of Praise* on BBC television. He was knighted in 1981 and from then on he often referred to himself as 'Sir Cumference'. Illness plagued his later life. He had two strokes and suffered from prostate cancer. Typical of the man, he made an inspiring TV documentary about how he dealt with his illnesses before he passed away in 2001 aged 79.

My regular weekly gigs at the Drake Inn and the Tudor Rooms helped raise my profile on the Dublin cabaret scene and soon I was being asked to appear all over the city. I had a great relationship with the promoters and the publicans for whom I worked and I rarely had a written contract. Once a year I would get together with people like John Lyons or Pat O'Donnell and we would agree on a deal that would last until the following year – all on the basis of a handshake.

Cabaret work was a lot more relaxed than constantly touring with the showbands. Even if I worked most nights of the week, I was home to Sheila and the children at a fairly respectable hour and I did not need to leave the house again until the next evening. This schedule also allowed me to make appearances with the RTÉ Light Orchestra where I would join up with great performers like Austin Gaffney, Des Smith and Anne Bushnell. Austin Gaffney was probably the best known tenor in the country at that time. He spent much of the year appearing as guest star in musicals all over Ireland and had mastered dozens of lead roles in shows like *The Desert Song, The New Moon,*

Annie Get Your Gun and *The Merry Widow*. His enormous fan base included every young lady who ever appeared in the chorus of an amateur musical production.

Austin also appeared regularly with Maureen Potter in her pantos and summer shows. Having learned her trade with the great Jimmy O'Dea, Maureen had become a 'national treasure' and her shows were booked out wherever she appeared. Every Summer she starred in a show called *Gaels of Laughter* which was produced by Fred O'Donovan at the Gaiety Theatre with a regular company that included Danny Cummins, Vernon Hayden and Jim Bartley, an actor who was to become my long-time friend. I first met Jim when I was given a spot on *Gaels of Laughter* and we hit it off from the very start. Fred O'Donovan put me on early in the show so that I could get away to my regular cabaret gigs but like the rest of the cast I had to dress up in a fancy costume for the opening number. Mine was a Harlequin suit, all polka dots and frills, fastened with buttons up the back. I knew that I needed a quick change before I went on stage for my spot so I got the idea of buttoning the suit up the front. It worked for most of the run, until one evening in the Green Room, Maureen was doing the rounds of the cast, encouraging them, easing their stage fright and making sure that they looked their best when they went on stage.

'Sonny, darling,' she said when she got to me, 'I'm afraid that your Harlequin costume is on back to front.'

Of course, there was no choice but to rectify the situation so every evening after that, Jim Bartley would have to help me into and out of the suit and it was often a matter of seconds between the unbuttoning and my walking on stage, smiling and pretending to be relaxed in my tuxedo. I was far from relaxed as I knew that every minute's delay would reduce the time I had

104   SONNY – *FOR THE GOOD TIMES*

to get to the Drake Inn or the Tudor Rooms – and very often it was touch and go. I enjoyed this little episode 'on the stage' and thought that Molly Coulihan would have been proud of me.

Jim Bartley, of course, went on to become one of Ireland's most talented and best-loved actors. He has appeared in scores of plays but is best loved for his television roles in *Tolka Row* and *Fair City*. Back in 1964, *Tolka Row* was Telefís Éireann's first soap and was based on a play by Maura Laverty. Jim was a regular member of the cast and played alongside Brenda Fricker who was later to win an Oscar for her performance in the film *My Left Foot*. In *Fair City*, Jim plays *Bella*, the doyen of the Doyle family, a role which has seen him feature in many dramatic and often tragic story lines. He has spoken to the media recently about his empathy with Bella who lost a child in the TV series. Playing the tragic scenes, he said, reminded him of his own feelings when his son Emmet died in 1987 following an asthma attack. Jim's trademark limp, incidentally, is the result of a football injury sustained in a showbiz football game many years ago. Another friend with a 'stage limp' was Joe Lynch who played Dinny in *Glenroe*. We first met in the USA when we toured with Ruby Murray in the 1950s. I was in The Earl Gill Band and Joe was the compere. He is best remembered as an actor but Joe was also a fine singer who made several records for Waltons in the Fifties including *The Wild Colonial Boy*. The records were played every week on the Waltons sponsored programme on Radio Éireann and the entire nation knew the oft-repeated slogan, 'If you feel like singing – DO sing an Irish song.' Joe came into his own in the radio series *Living With Lynch,* which featured Pamela Duncan, Ronnie Walsh and another Maureen Potter sidekick, Charlie Byrne, who was MC at the Shamrock Ballroom in New York when I played there in the Sixties. Joe was the star of the show which created catchphrases which are still used today – 'Ya heard it before Joe' and 'What about the workin' man?' The most famous quote attributed to Joe (a proud Corkonian) came when he was asked about his loyalty to the county hurling team.

'I love Cork so much,' he said, 'that if I caught one of their hurlers in bed with my missus, I'd tiptoe down the stairs and make him a cup of tea.'

Joe sadly passed away in Spain in 2001.

The thing I remember most about the Gaiety shows is the fabulous costumes which everybody got to wear. I have always liked nice clothes (it must be the tailor in me) and I suppose I have moved with the fashions over the years. In the early days with Joe Coughlan and Earl Gill, we dressed like waiters – formal dress suits and black bows – not very different from the dress suits my father wore when he went off to work from Chancery Lane. The showband era saw us, first of all, wearing blazers and slacks and, later on, colourful showband suits. The Pacific had very nice red blazers and white slacks with several changes of costume over my period in the band. Cabaret however required something different and I began to wear velvet jackets with wide lapels, flared trousers and platform soled shoes. I always had a good mop of hair and in the Seventies I grew it down to my shoulders, which was all the fashion at the time. Indeed in a family portrait which hangs on our wall at home, both my son Gary and I look very proud of our flowing locks. I grew a moustache also around that time and kept it until recently, although as I moved on in life, it was trimmed a bit shorter than it was in the Seventies.

For a long time I was mainly a Dublin entertainer, working almost every night of the week and frequently doing two or even three shows on any given night. My first move out of the capital was when I got a call from Donal Bourke in Cork who invited me to play down there. I told him that I was virtually unknown outside of Dublin but he insisted.

'Come on down and give it a go, Horatio,' he said. (For some reason that he never explained, he always called me 'Horatio'.) I agreed to do a show at Moore's Hotel and it was a sellout – so I went back there regularly. This encouraged me to play other venues also and I did many shows in Cruise's and the Royal George hotels in Limerick. My most regular accompanist, then and over many years, is Paudge Griffin – an amazing musician who plays any keyboard instrument and who knows my repertoire like the back of his hand. We still play together and when Paudge is around, I know that I am in good hands.

These were marvellous years. I was busy, successful and enjoying my singing. The venues were small enough to enable me to communicate with the audience and people would regularly come up to me to chat or even bring me a drink. I never used recorded backing tracks and preferred to work with professional musicians that I had known for years. One of the advantages was that if somebody came up to the stage with a request, I could break off and talk to them. The band would 'mark time' and would pick up the tune again when I was ready to resume. You could not do that with a karaoke machine.

As I matured in style and age, so did my audience. The kids who jived to The Capitol Showband now had grown-up families and often grandchildren.

As a fan put it to me one evening:

'Ah – you're one of our own, Sonny. You're the Mick Jagger of the Grannies.'

Tony Kenny ...
'Friends for Life'

Some years ago *The Sunday Tribune* ran a series of features called *Friends for Life* in which they invited pairs of people to talk about their mutual friendship. I was paired with Sonny Knowles – and it could not have been a better choice.

My first contact with Sonny was when I was leaving The Sands Showband to pursue a career as a solo performer. At that stage, Sonny was the 'King of Cabaret' in Dublin and somebody every musician and performer in the city greatly admired. I bucked up the courage to call him to ask for advice and I received a typically warm and friendly welcome. He talked about his own career and experiences and then came up with a piece of advice that had nothing to do with singing or performing or promotion. 'Keep the tax man happy and you will be fine,' he advised. It was a sound piece of advice that I have tried to follow over the years.

As I began to develop my own career, I heard tales of the legendary Sonny Knowles, who seemed to have the gift of bi-location or multi-location because he would do cabaret spots at several venues on the same night. It was possible to meet people who would tell you that they had been at his show in Finglas, Terenure and the city centre on the same Friday or Saturday.

We first met up in RTÉ when we were both cast in a Jack Cruise

Christmas Panto. It was *Aladdin* and I was in the title role with Sonny playing the role of the Emperor. I still remember his elaborate costume and formidable long moustache. We hit it off immediately, helped by the fact that we were both from the Liberties. I lived at Carman's Hall off Francis Street and Sonny was from Chancery Lane behind Dublin Castle. We had lots to talk about, knew many of the same people and became instant good friends.

From then onwards we met regularly. My wife Joan and I would meet up with Sonny and Sheila on holidays in Spain and we would get together at charity events. I can say sincerely that no artiste that I know has done more for charity than Sonny Knowles. Over the years I have known him, he has always been to the fore in volunteering his unique talent to help a good cause. We have performed together at VATS and Variety Club events and we even made a single record for charity. It was a duet version of *Hey, Won't You Play Another Somebody Done Somebody Wrong Song* (which must be one of the longest song titles ever recorded) and we also performed medleys together.

It was an honour for me to invite Sonny to guest on some of my shows and whenever he appeared he would 'bring the house down'. People just loved him – and still do. From the moment he walks on stage, he establishes a warmth and rapport with his audience that is unrivalled on the Irish entertainment scene.

He also has the unique ability to deliver a polished and professional performance irrespective of the accompaniment. It doesn't matter to Sonny whether the musicians behind him are the National Concert Orchestra or a waiter banging on a tray – he can still deliver a first class show. Nor indeed does the venue matter. I have watched him sing in small pubs and at big venues like the Helix or the National Concert Hall, and the connection which he creates with the audience is always the same.

I believe that Sonny is, first and foremost, a musician. He began his musical career playing the saxophone and clarinet in the dance orchestras of the Fifties and has played alongside some of the finest musicians in the country in groups as diverse as The Earl Gill Band and the National Concert Orchestra. It is this musicianship which is the foundation of his talent as an entertainer, and on to this he has built a polished singing style, a precise sense of timing, but most of all, his own open, warm and friendly personality.

He is blessed with these talents, but also with his lovely wife Sheila who has been at his side from the very beginning of his career and particularly through the recent traumatic years of illness.

Sonny's remarkable comeback and the success he enjoys today have brought great joy to Sheila, their family, Sonny's thousands of fans and admirers, to Joan and to me.

I am indeed proud that we are 'Friends for Life'.

CHAPTER **8**

Checkpoint Charlie

reland's love affair with the Eurovision Song Contest began
in 1970 when Dana won the competition with *All Kinds of
Everything*. This was the beginning of an amazing run for this
country, which first entered Eurovision in 1965 with Butch
Moore singing *I'm Walking the Streets in the Rain*. We had to
wait ten years for our second success with Johnny Logan
winning in 1980, singing Shay Healy's song *What's Another
Year?* Johnny won again in 1987 with his own song *Hold Me
Now* and he completed a remarkable hat trick in 1992 as
composer of *Why Me?* which was sung by Linda Martin and
again won the competition. The hat trick continued with Niamh
Kavanagh winning in the following year with *In Your Eyes*

written by Jimmy Walsh. Paul Harrington and Charlie McGettigan made it three in a row in 1994 with a great song *Rock'n'Roll Kids*, written by Brendan Graham who also wrote *The Voice* which was a winner for Eimear Quinn in 1996.

Since then, of course, the Eurovision Song Contest has changed beyond recognition, with the emphasis on productions rather than on songs. This trend, and a combination of 'good neighbour' voting, has kept us out of the winners' enclosure – but we can hardly complain as we remain one of the most successful countries in the history of the competition.

My own involvement in Eurovision was peripheral. I did backing vocals for some of the National Song Contest entries and I played in the orchestra when Eurovision was staged in the Gaiety Theatre in 1971. It was an interesting experience because we were directed by more than a dozen conductors from all over Europe. The arrangements were sent to Dublin in advance and we rehearsed them under the direction of Noel Kelehan. The artists arrived during the week of the contest and we had long days of rehearsal as they all went through their acts. Finally on the night, the show went out live to an audience of more than 300 million people and a series of visiting musical directors stepped up in turn to conduct the various songs. We had to get it right first time and to our credit, we did.

While I never represented Ireland in Eurovision, I did so at a series of song contests held in Eastern Europe. This was during the Cold War and the Berlin Wall was still firmly in place. Very few people from Western Europe crossed the 'Iron Curtain', the virtual border between the democracies of the West and the Communist states of the East, Around 1975 however, I was approached by Michael Geoghegan, a good friend, with an offer I just could not refuse. He invited me to travel to Split in

Yugoslavia (now in Croatia) to perform at a song contest there. All my expenses would be paid and (here was the clincher) I could bring Sheila along for the trip. We talked it over and the prospect of a free holiday was very appealing. These song contests were highly popular across Eastern Europe and were probably established as an alternative to Eurovision, which did not allow Communist countries to compete. They had an interesting format which involved a local artist singing a song in the local language and then a visiting artist singing the same song in English. I was sent the words and music for three songs. The lyrics were translated into English by Tony McNeill and I learned the songs before flying out to the contest. I would also sing other songs, which would not be familiar to the audience during the event. They did however know *Greensleeves* which was the theme of a television show which could be picked up in Eastern Europe. Not all songs were acceptable to the authorities however and one of mine called *Music from Across the Way*, was on the banned list.

We had a marvelous time in Split. The sun shone, the scenery was spectacular, the people were warm and welcoming and we lived in luxury in the Hotel Lam. Better still, my song was placed third in the contest. Sheila and I went back to Split many years later on holiday and it was wonderful to sit in a café in the same square where I had competed in the song contest. The city had not changed very much and remains as beautiful as ever.

Among the people we met in Split was Manfred Nietschke, who invited us to a similar song contest in Dresden. On the basis of our experience in Split, we accepted the invitation, not knowing anything much about the city. We were scheduled to fly to Dresden via London but when we were flying to London to pick up the flight, a problem arose on our aircraft and it had to return to Dublin. As a result we missed our London connection and had to fly to West Berlin instead. We were then faced with the prospect of going through Checkpoint Charlie so we hired a taxi to take us to the border. Checkpoint Charlie was an eerie place, with West German guards on one side and East German guards on the other. It was illuminated by bright floodlights and protected by a high wall and razor-wire fencing. Nasty-looking dogs strained on their leashes, every guard had a gun at the ready and mirrors on little trolleys were pushed under the wheels of every vehicle to check for possible refugees. When we got there, we were in for a shock for we discovered that we needed visas to get into East Berlin – and we did not have them. We were put into a black car and driven from one checkpoint to the next. And there we waited, as stern border guards talked for a long time on the telephone. At one point I got out of the car to stretch my legs – but I was quickly ordered to get back inside. Eventually it was sorted out and we were brought through to a waiting taxi which took us on the two-hour journey to Dresden. When we told our story afterwards, people marvelled about how we managed to get through Checkpoint Charlie without visas.

Over the next few years I participated in five similar song contests in Eastern Europe including memorable visits to Prague in what was then Czechoslovakia and Karl Marx Stadt, a city in Saxony, which is now known as Chemnitz. We were well received everywhere. The theatres were of a very high quality and no expense was spared by the Communist governments when it came to promoting culture. Sheila and I stayed in the best of hotels and when I performed it was often with an 80-piece orchestra conducted by people like Jurgen Herman.

After one performance in a large theatre, the audience began to slow hand-clap in unison. I said to myself, 'Jaysus – that didn't go down too well,' but the stage manager was all smiles and congratulations. 'That is how we respond to a wonderful performance,' he explained.

The people were somewhat more reserved than the Irish but they were always polite and courteous. Inevitably there were a few exceptions such as the wife of one of our hosts who told us one evening at dinner that she was 'very romantic'. Describing her plans for the evening, she said: 'I eat, I drink, I love, I sleep.'

We were free to explore the cities that we visited and the organisers provided us with a guide/interpreter in the person of Gerhard Kleiner, a harpist in the orchestra who worked as a guide during his spare time. He became a good friend and we would specially ask for him to be our interpreter whenever we visited Eastern Europe, There was no shortage of museums, palaces and art galleries to visit but shopping was very limited. It largely comprised highly specialised shops which might sell jumpers or shoes or overcoats. Only a limited number of shoppers would be allowed into the store at any one time. Each was given a basket and the security staff knew how many people were shopping by counting the baskets that remained. The police were never far away and one evening we were stopped while walking in Karl Marx Stadt. We had no papers with us so I explained what we were doing with the word 'singen' (meaning 'singing'), which was one of the few German words I knew. It took some time for them to understand but when they did, their demeanour changed and, with a smile, they sent us on our way.

These song contests were held before the age of video and I regret that we don't have any visual souvenirs. We did take photographs but again there were controls on what pictures we could take. On one occasion Sheila was standing in the wings of a theatre while I was performing and she aimed her camera at me. A security person immediately intervened to stop her. Sheila explained that she just wanted a picture of me on stage and the security lady eventually relented but specified the precise angle at which the picture could be taken. Apparently leading members of the Politburo were sitting in the front row and it was not allowed to take their picture.

Other tours enabled me to travel elsewhere in Europe and to the USA. On one occasion we were in Roosevelt Field in New York where my good friend, the comedian Noel V. Ginnity (known to us as 'Noddy') was in the show. I went to buy some v-neck vests which were on sale there. They could be worn inside an open-neck shirt without being seen. They came in packs of three and I bought a pack. I then thought that maybe I would need a few more so I asked for a second pack. When I asked for a third pack, Noel who was renowned for having a 'short fuse' intervened.

'Jaysus Sonny,' he said in his distinctive voice, 'You'll be dead before you wear that lot out.'

Happily, he was wrong.

Back home, my cabaret work continued to prosper. I was much in demand for spots in pubs, cabaret rooms and dinner dances. The Green Isle Hotel ran a very popular dinner dance on Saturday nights, which attracted people from all over Dublin. It was a great value evening with a good meal, a cabaret show and a dance until 1am. I was a regular cabaret performer there and would often arrive very close to the deadline, having already sung in one or even two different venues across the city. After one show I met up with Tommy Ellis who ran a recording studio in Mount Street and he suggested that I should think about making an LP. It would be a good means of promoting my cabaret act, he suggested. As a result I was introduced to Rego Records, which claims to be 'the world's oldest publisher, distributor and manufacturer of Irish music'. Many well-known Irish acts recorded for the label, which had a large market in the UK and continues to distribute Irish music to US buyers over the Internet. My first LP therefore was geared to this audience and included songs like *Annaghdown, When Your Old Wedding Ring Was New, Dublin Saunter, Banks of My Old Lovely Lee, The Dying Rebel, Rose of Mooncoin* and *When I Leave the World Behind*, a song that remains in my repertoire today.

From a promotional point of view, it made more sense for me to record for the Irish market and I switched to Michael Geoghegan's Rex Records, which was a division of Decca, for my next album. It was called *Tell Me* and it included several fine arrangements by Johnny Tate. Over the next few years I was a frequent visitor to recording studios both in Dublin and London and I completed eight LPs spanning a wide range of music. One of the first, called simply *Sonny Knowles,* included tracks like the Charles Aznavour song *Dance in the Old Fashioned Way*, Phil Coulter's very moving *Scorn Not His Simplicity* which I still like to sing, the famous *Three Good Reasons* which I had copied from Frank Ifield, my Pacific Showband hits No *One Knows* and No *One Will Ever Know* and even Kris Kristofferson's *Help Me Make It Through the Night* The late Kevin Marron, a brilliant journalist who worked for the *Sunday Press* and later the *Sunday World* and who was to die tragically in an airline accident, wrote the sleeve note for that LP during which he recalled an evening at the Drake Inn.

'The last time I saw him (Sonny) perform was in the Drake Inn, Finglas, where he has the kind of support Liverpool have in The Kop. As well as his usual song spot, he was also master

of ceremonies. His duties that night included introducing a well-known international artiste who makes more appearances in newspapers than she does on stage. She didn't appear that night and it fell to Sonny to break the news to a house that had paid a hefty cover charge and had made it to Finglas through a busless Dublin. It says a lot for his special kind of popularity that the news was greeted with indifference. It says a lot for his modesty that he was scared they would lynch him. It says even more for his talent that he sang a few more songs and sent them home happy.'

The singer in question was Kathy Kirby who had a long-running alcohol problem.

Wind in My Hands, a Paul Brady song, was the title track on another album, which included some of my all time favourites, like *Roses of Picardy* and *I'll Take Care of Your Cares*. Other tracks included *My Child* and the Tom Jones hit *Isadora*.

Liam Nolan, who was a distinguished broadcaster and the Pat Kenny of his day, wrote the sleeve note for another LP called *Memory Lane*. Liam was a keen boxing fan and referred to my short boxing career in his piece. The album was notable for a few reasons. I played alto sax on *Just the Way You Are*, baritone sax on *Beginning to See the Light,* as well as clarinet on a Twenties medley that included old favourites like *If You Knew Susie, Margie, Dinah and Sweet Georgia Brown*. We also included an original Jim Doherty song called *Then and Now*. Jim produced the LP and was responsible for several of the arrangements. My favourite track from that LP was *Shaney Boy*, a lovely song by the Australian singer-songwriter Kevin Johnson who also wrote *Rock and Roll I Gave You The Best Years of My Life*, which was a firm favourite with Val Joyce over the years. *Shaney Boy* is all about a young son growing up and it

118

struck a chord with me because at the time my own son Gary was growing into adulthood. I am sure all fathers will relate to the lines:

'And the morning passes quickly in our lifetime
And before you even notice, it's gone
So, little boy, I'm noticing the nice times now
'Cos I know that little boys don't stay little boys for long.'

On some LPs I was a guest rather than the featured artist. These included an early album with Family Pride and another with a group called The Ruby Singers which included Des Smith, John Curran and Johnny Christopher. You won't find any mention of Sonny Knowles on this LP as I ran into some contractual difficulties and sang under the pseudonym 'Gary Austin'. I do however appear on the cover, well disguised in a Stetson bearing the legend 'Marshal', shades, neckerchief and pink shirt – and holding a GUITAR!. The album had some nice tracks such as *The Bowery Grenadiers. Along Came Jones, Try a Little Kindness, Lagan Love* and a 'Spanish' medley of *Harlem, Eyes and Lace.* One of my solos on the album was a lovely song, written by John Lennon and Paul McCartney, called *If I Fell (in Love with You).* It provided me with a rare occasion to record a Beatles song. The album was produced by Jerry Hughes and the arrangements were all by John Curran. Ruby Records, which distributed the album, was based in Donnybrook and also recorded Margo, Dermot Henry, The Smokeys, Des and Johnny Kelly (ex Capitol Showband) and an album featuring Jerry Hughes himself.

I was also featured on a 1981 LP by the Dublin Concert Band and the Glasnevin Musical Society, which had an introduction by Gay Byrne. This time however I had secured permission from my then record label Polygram to play instrumentals with the band and I was soloist on two tracks – the Burt Bacharach song *Alfie,* and *Cavatina* which was featured in the film *The Deer Hunter.* This LP was interesting because it was the first Irish-produced album in a format called 'Binaural Stereo'. It was designed to be heard through headphones and would deliver a 'surround sound' which was close to that experienced at a live performance. The technical innovation employed was that, in the process of recording, microphones would be placed so that they received sound at precisely the same moment as it would be heard by the ear of an audience member. Other stereo systems of the time relied solely on sound differences to create a stereophonic reception.

In choosing songs for these albums I was more attracted to the artistes who had recorded them rather than the songwriters. I was a huge fan of artistes like Eddy Arnold, who was known as 'The Tennessee Plowboy', Perry Como and of course, Max Bygraves who, like myself, was a master of the medley. Max was born in the London docklands, son of a professional boxer who was known as 'Battling Tom Smith'. A boy soprano, who was a soloist at Westminster Cathedral, he worked in an advertising agency and as a carpenter before going off to war with the RAF. He frequently entertained his comrades during the War and when it was over, he was invited by the BBC to sing in a celebration concert alongside Frankie Howerd, Benny Hill, Jimmy Edwards, my good friend Harry Secombe and Spike Milligan. This led to other gigs. He appeared at the London Palladium in 1951, was given a spot on the Royal Command Performance Variety Show and supported Judy Garland in New York. Max was an actor and comedian as well as a singer and he coined a number of memorable catchphrases such as 'I want to tell you a story...', 'A good idea, son' and 'I've arrived – and to prove it I'm here.' He also had spots on BBC radio shows like *Educating Archie* and appeared in several films including *Bless 'Em All, Skimpy in the Navy, Tom Brown's Schooldays, A Cry from the Streets* and *Charley Moon* in which he played the title role.

For me however, it was his recordings that made me a big fan, particularly the hugely successful *Singalongamax* series of albums which included scores of tunes. Max had a long list of hit singles from 1958 to 1989 including *The Gang That Sang Heart of My Heart* (1954), *Mr. Sandman* (1955), *Meet Me on the Corner* (1955), *The Ballad of Davy Crockett* (1956), *Tulips from Amsterdam* and *You Need Hands* (1958), *Fings Ain't Wot They Used T'be* (1960), *Consider Yourself* (1960), *You're My Everything* (1969) and the monologue *Deck of Cards* (1973). In 1954 he also recorded what must have been the pop song with the longest ever title – *Gilly Gilly Ossenfeffer Katzenellen Bogen by the Sea*. Max retired a few times but he was still performing in public in 2006 when he toured the UK with great success. He now lives in Queensland and hopefully is still working away on a few new medleys.

I am deeply indebted to him, not only for the listening pleasure which he has brought me over the years, but also for the enormous contribution which he has made to my repertoire.

Thank you Max.

As you might say yourself – 'I'm alive – and to prove it, I'm here.'

Paul O'Reilly ...
'Three Good Reasons to Love Sonny'

Sonny was a household name in the early 1970s when I first started working in my father's shop, *Dolphin Discs,* in Marlborough Street. It was around this time that the showband scene was beginning to fade and the cabaret scene was becoming more popular, particularly in Dublin.

Sonny was a very successful artist and we sold large quantities of his singles and albums at the time. I met him twice back then – once with Michael Geoghegan, MD of Irish Record Factors, who distributed Sonny's albums. On the other occasion, he came into our shop and it caused great excitement. There were a lot of fruit sellers on the street outside and as soon as they heard that Sonny was in Dolphin, a large crowd congregated both inside and outside the shop. He responded with surprise and genuine warmth to their unbridled adulation and it was obvious that the crowd really loved him.

When the idea of releasing a collection of Sonny's hits came up in 2007, I knew immediately that it would be a great album. I met Sonny with Pat Egan to progress the project and then, together with Ronan Collins and my brother Ger who also works in retail, we put together a list of suggested tracks.

I compiled *The Best of ...* over the Summer of 2007, listening to Sonny's songs as I drove to and from Brittas Bay many times with my seven year-old daughter Eva. She would always request the Sonny Knowles 'One, Two, Three' song (*Three Good Reasons* to give it its correct title) and proceed to sing along. It seems there is a whole new generation waiting to discover and enjoy Sonny's superb and timeless recordings.

Harry Bradshaw, with many years of experience, transferred the vinyl tracks to CD and we were both amazed at the quality of the sound production on the tracks, even though they had been recorded back in the 1970s. The arrangements and orchestrations are fantastic; as good as anything you'd hear recorded today.

There is a very special quality about Sonny's voice and he has always had a great talent for choosing wonderful songs. I remember telling him that a particular favourite of mine is called *The Only Couple on the Floor* because it reminds me of the first time I danced with my wife Katie. Or should I say, the first time I had a 'lurch' with her. He laughed and said, 'We call that the "broken bed song!"'

Another factor in his great success is that he's such a lovely, humble man with a great, natural warmth, which I think comes across in his songs and live performances. Sonny is probably one of the easiest artists I've ever dealt with, a joy to work with and always so enthusiastic.

We released the album *The Very Best of Sonny Knowles* in 2007 and there was an unbelievable reaction to it. It sold Platinum for Christmas and the second album *Sonny – The Love Songs Collection* was also a great success in 2008.

When it comes to album signings in record shops, there is always a worry that nobody will turn up. When Sonny appeared in Dolphin Discs on Moore Street for the launch of *The Very Best of ...,* we had a huge turnout, even though it was raining heavily. It was clear from their reaction that everyone still loved Sonny, though I think even he was taken aback at how many people were there.

I think that part of the reason for his success is that the songs he chose were timeless. When we're all long gone, Sonny's songs will still be heard and for me it was a privilege to be involved with such an iconic artist.

CHAPTER **9**

All That Jazz

From a very early age I had an interest in and a love for jazz. Growing up in Drimnagh, I listened to the music of Glen Miller, Tommy Dorsey, Count Basie, Duke Ellington, Joe Loss, Ted Heath and other big bands on the radio and I was always impressed by the way the music was arranged by the impromptu playing of the soloists. Another favourite was Ray McVay from Scotland who toured Ireland regularly. His trombone player was Bobby Burns from Cabra who sang in the style of Perry Como and was a very good friend of mine. His brother Paddy was also a musician and played with Eileen Reid and the Cadets.

When I joined the Post Office Workers Band, I met up with musicians who were also into the big band scene and several of the teachers at Dublin School of Music were also keen jazz players. Earl Gill, of course, was one of the top jazz musicians in the country at that time and I learned a lot about phrasing and improvisation when I played in his band. This was also the era of British Trad and bands like Chris Barber, Terry Lightfoot, Acker Bilk, Kenny Ball and Humphrey Lyttleton found themselves in the pop charts as well as packing out venues like the Marquee Club in London. Most of them also toured Ireland and a few are still going strong. Chris Barber was the first to popularise Dixieland or 'Trad Jazz' in Britain. He was a charismatic band leader and a fine trombone player and he surrounded himself with some very talented musicians including Lonnie Donegan, who played banjo with Chris and later introduced skiffle to a new audience. Scottish-born Lonnie had a long series of hits including *My Old Man's a Dustman, Rock Island Line, Tom Dooley, Does Your Chewing Gum Lose Its Flavour on the Bedpost Overnight, Battle of New Orleans, San Miguel* and *Nobody Loves Like an Irishman,* which naturally went down well on his Irish tours. Ottilie Patterson, who was married to Chris, was the featured singer in the band. Ottilie was from Comber, Co. Down and was one of the finest jazz singers to come from this country. Other members of the band included Ken Colyer who had played in New Orleans and was regarded as the 'father' of British Trad, Pat Halcox on trumpet, Jim Bray on bass, Ronnie Bowden on drums and Monty Sunshine on clarinet. Monty gave the band a major instrumental hit with his version of the Sidney Bechet tune *Petite Fleur.*

The British Trad scene encouraged dance bands here to include Dixieland numbers in their sets and I often jammed away happily in The Earl Gill Band on old favourites like *High Society, Sweet Georgia Brown* and *When the Saints Go Marching In.* Some of these numbers were set pieces in which the solos had to be learned. For instance, the famous clarinet solo on *High Society* was (and still is) played as it was first written by Alphonse Picou in New Orleans back in 1901. He had adapted the tune from a march of the same name in which the solo appeared as an 'obligatto' for the piccolo.

I liked the idea of improvisation but never really had the talent to be a star jazz soloist. I tended to confine myself to reading scores or playing Dixieland and never got into the bop or modern jazz scenes. I have always admired jazz improvisers and still love to listen to the playing of sax players like Richie and Michael Buckley, pianists like Jim Doherty and Noel Kelehen and of course the great guitarist Louis Stewart. I have had the honour of playing with most of them over the years, sometimes in a jazz context but also in cabaret shows, recordings or concerts. Jim Doherty led several big bands who played at venues like the South County Hotel in Stillorgan and I often sat in with him and musicians like Rory McGuinness, Rock Fox, John Wadham and Dave Fleming. Jim had a small jazz group which played in the Martello Room on the top floor of Jurys Hotel in Ballsbridge. This was a sophisticated late night restaurant at the time and attracted the Dublin 'glitterati' of the day. He invited me to join them on occasions and it was a gig that I always enjoyed. I was also part of the RTÉ Big Band, again led by Jim, which performed at the Proms series of concerts in the RDS in the Eighties. The concerts were broadcast on RTÉ television and many of the arrangements were by Johnny Devlin, a superb musician and arranger. He was the musical director in bands which played at international music festivals and he had the ability to communicate with artistes, musicians and technicians from several European countries – all in their own language. Johnny was fluent in at least seven languages, was exceptionally well read and a true 'Renaissance Man'.

Dance orchestra members also liked to play jazz as a form of recreation and we would gather in the '55 Club' off O'Connell Street every week for an informal session. Up to 20 musicians could be there at any one time and we took turns playing in the band. I might sit in on baritone for a half hour or so and then wander off to the bar to allow another sax player to take over my seat. A few singers would also come along and on occasions the sessions would be of a very high standard. Unfortunately no audience ever got to hear them.

My happiest jazz memory of the Sixties, however, was one in which I did not play a note. On one memorable evening we went along to my old haunt at the National Boxing Stadium to see and hear the great Louis 'Satchmo' Armstrong and his All Stars. The ropes around the ring were removed and the band played from a platform in the middle of the stadium. Louis was probably the greatest jazz trumpeter of all time and he was treated like royalty whenever he went on tour. His band that evening featured some of the greatest traditional jazz musicians of the day, such as Ed Hall on clarinet, Trummy Young on trombone, Arvell Shaw on bass and Barrett Deems on drums. Satchmo played all the Dixieland favourites such as a mile-a-minute version of *Tiger Rag* and sang tunes like *The Faithful Hussar* in his gravelly voice, as well as playing the trumpet in his own unique style with soaring high notes and a wonderful golden tone.

That concert remains a happy memory not only of a magical musician but also of the National Stadium, which was built in 1939 as a boxing venue but also over the years has provided an intimate setting for concerts by (among many others) Cliff Richard, Leonard Cohen, James Last, Status Quo and Sting.

A sunny Sonny.

I particularly like this picture of Sheila.

Meeting President Mary McAleese at Áras on Úachtaráin.

Launching a pension plan for musicians with Louis Stewart and Earl Gill.

The "Window Washer" in action.

In ermine for my 60th Birthday.

Earl Gill, Richie Buckley, myself and Paddy Cole playing at my surprise 60th. Birthday Party in O'Connell Street, Dublin The party was broadcast live on the 'Gay Byrne Show' on RTE Radio One.

With Sheila in New York, when I was named 'New York Dubliner of the Year'.

Singing on the RTE 'Live at Three' show

With Sheila at the VATS 'Hall of Fame Award'.

Blowing my baritone sax at the Kinsale Jazz Festival.

Me singing and Ronan Collins drumming.

With Sheila and the Lord Mayor of Cork, Dan Wallace, when I was declared an 'Honorary Citizen of Cork'.

Performing Artistes Trust Society

Founded 1969

✶ ✶ ✶ ✶

Presents

THE LIVING LEGEND AWARD
to
SONNY KNOWLES

WHERE HIS SHOWBIZ COLLEAGUES WILL PAY SPECIAL TRIBUTE TO HIM, IN A STAR STUDDED CABARET SHOW

Johnny Carroll

Clair Rooney

Sean Dunphy

Des Smith

Euro Big Band

Sil Fox

Dave Young

Jim Farrelly

Tony Kenny

Rory O'Connor Dancers

Al Banim

Dale King

Earl Gill

June Rogers

Plus Surprise Guest Appearances

In Citywest Hotel on Sun. 9th Sept. 2007
8pm till 1am • Doors open at 7pm

PRODUCED & PRESENTED BY PATRICIA DUFFY & BRIAN O'CONNOR • STAGE MANAGER, PAT O'DONNELL

MUSIC BY STREETWISE. COMPERE, JOE CUDDY.

TICKETS AVAILABLE FROM: Patricia: 087 2359040 or 01 8203229. Bridie: 01 8474839.
Brian: 01 8214603. Maureen: 01 4519972 or 087 6359604.
OB1 Menswear, Unit 40, Ilac Centre. Ph: 01 8733646.
Crumlin Glass Co. Crumlin Village. Office hours Ph: 01 4550199.
A Team Newsagents, 21 St. Agnes Road, Crumlin. Ph: 01 4555373.
The Tallaght Pet Shop, Tallaght Village. Ph: 01 4599466.
FOR CREDIT CARD BOOKINGS PHONE 01 8203229
SOUND SPONSORED BY TERRY HERON AUDIO SERVICES.
• ADMISSION €25 & €35 •
OVERNIGHT ACCOMMODATION IF REQUIRED MAY BE BOOKED DIRECTLY WITH CITYWEST
HOTEL AT A COST OF €110 PER SINGLE ROOM OR €140 PER DOUBLE ROOM

ALL PROCEEDS TO THE P.A.T.S. BENEVOLENT FUND

Poster for the PATS 'Living Legend' evening, which raised a large sum for charity.

With Marco Petrassi and Paddy Cole in Kinsale.

Sonny with journalist Andrea Smith (left) and Paul O'Reilly of Dolphin Records.

Our grandchildren. From left are Raymond, Hayley, Kenny, Lorna and Alan.

Geraldine, Gary and Aisling pictured this year in Australia.

Sheila and I with Butch Moore.

In my early cabaret days.

In my Pacific Showband days.

An RTE Guide cover promoting my 'Cabaret' television show.

Sonny on Talk of the Town with Pat O'Donnell, Entertainment Manager, Slattery's Terenure

On holidays in Malta with Sheila, 2009

Me today!

Dublin has always had a lively jazz scene and over the years, I played with some fine musicians at a variety of venues, including the Green Room on St. Stephen's Green which had a regular weekly session featuring Rock Fox, Dara O'Loughlin, Rory McGuinness, Noel Kelehan and others.

My most lasting jazz gig has been in Kinsale, where I have played at the Cork Fringe Jazz Festival for the past 15 years. This long and happy association began when I was doing a cabaret show in Actons Hotel, Kinsale, backed by trumpet player Marco Petrassi and his band. I was out on the dance floor, singing away, when one of the band members, for no apparent reason, handed me a tenor sax and a sling. 'What am I to do with this?' I asked in a whisper, 'I haven't played a sax in years.' 'Give it a go,' he whispered back. I tried rapidly to remember even one tune I could play and decided to have a go at *Bill Bailey* and *Jambalaya*. Somehow or other, I got through this 'instrumental' and went back to what I knew I could do – I sang another medley.

After the show I was introduced to Billy Crosbie of the famous *Cork Examiner* newspaper family who is also a talented jazz pianist. Almost immediately he invited me to Kinsale for the next Cork Jazz Festival. 'I don't know if I could play jazz at this level after a gap of so many years,' I protested. 'Oh yes – you can,' said Billy, 'I heard the way you played those two tunes and it was pure jazz.'

So I had little option but to accept the invitation – and after 15 years, I have not yet been sacked.

The Cork Jazz Festival is known wherever jazz is played and enjoyed, and today that means most of the world. It was first held in 1978 when Jim Mountjoy, sales and marketing manager at the Metropole Hotel, found that he had a lot of empty beds over the October Bank Holiday because a bridge congress had been cancelled. He hit on the idea of attracting jazz fans and engaged some local bands to play over the weekend. The event was a big success and it encouraged Jim to expand the festival in the following year. Players-Wills came on board as a sponsor and the John Player Cork International Jazz Festival was born. Over the following years, Jim and a local organising committee were given a handsome budget by Players-Wills to attract the biggest names in jazz to Cork. They were outstandingly successful in signing up stars like Ella Fitzgerald, Oscar Peterson, Dizzy Gillespie, Mel Torme, Billy Eckstein, The Modern Jazz Quartet, Cleo Laine and John Dankworth. When Players bowed out in 1982, Guinness took over both the sponsorship and the operation of the festival, involving scores of Cork pubs in the event and promoting it in their overseas markets. Once again the budget allowed festival manager Jack McGouran to bring the finest jazz talents to Cork and over the years the guest list has read like a 'Who's Who' of jazz greats, including Lionel Hampton, Buddy Rich, Gerry Mulligan, Dave Brubeck, Wynton Marsalis, Sonny Rollins and many more.

Anecdotes about the festival abound and are often retold by musicians and festival goers. One concerns the blind pianist George Shearing, who was persuaded to play in the village of Blarney after an enterprising hotel manager had sent him an invitation in Braille. A second concerns the American guitarist Barney Kessel who walked up to the reception desk at his hotel and drawled 'Barney Kessel'. The Cork receptionist thought he had said 'Blarney Castle' and very helpfully advised him to go outside the door and hail a taxi and that it was a journey of about ten miles. The one I like best however is when a top act pulled out through illness and the organisers had to look around hastily to find a replacement, which they did in the person of the very elegant chanteuse Adelaide Hall. A delighted manager passed this good news to the Guinness Festival Director who responded: 'OK, we have Adelaide Hall. Now where do we find a band to play there?'

I enjoyed playing at the Cork Jazz Festival, particularly in a Sunday morning session at the Powdermill Bar in Ballincollig where the band would include Don Long, formerly the trombone player with The Capitol Showband, Paddy Cole on clarinet and sax, Joe Mac of The Dixies on drums and Billy Crosbie on piano. This gig came about as a result of playing in the Fringe Festival in Kinsale which remains marvelous fun. The house band which plays at Actons Hotel over the long weekend is known variously as The Cork City Jazz Band or Billy Crosbie and Friends and includes Cork trumpet player Marco Petrassi, a great character and splendid musician. His Italian father introduced him to the mandolin and he also played accordion before taking up the trumpet after hearing recordings by the great Harry James. He is renowned for his stamina and can blow at a session for several hours on end. The lineup also includes Jack Brierley on piano. Jack was a member of the Regal Showband in the Fifties and later led his own Jack Brierley Showband. He is a very talented composer and has written many songs with George Crosbie who was a director of *The Cork Examiner* and who sadly passed away this year. They came second in the National Song Contest in 1968 with the appropriately titled song *Kinsale* and won the competition in 1973 with *Do I Dream?* which was performed at Eurovision in Luxembourg by my great friend Maxi. Paddy Cole is also a regular at Kinsale, although for many years he was resident at the Blarney Park Hotel during the festival. Paddy is something of a legend on the Irish music scene and in his native Castleblayney. His All Stars have been playing to packed houses all over the country since the 1970s and are as fresh sounding today as they were at their first gig. Another great character in the band is Frank Ireland, who despite his name was born in the East End of London. A man of military bearing who flourishes an RAF moustache, he was a gunnery instructor in the Middle East when the RAF band called him into their ranks and he went on to play with them in many parts of the world. Frank also played with the Syd Deane Orchestra, which was based in Brighton and which made more than 500 broadcasts of music in the Glen Miller style. Since moving to Cork in 1988, he has been a Kinsale regular.

The Crosbie family is, of course, well represented in the band with the ebullient Billy on piano and vocalists Susan and Sharon Crosbie. Sharon was an opera singer before she turned to jazz, while Susan began her career in London before returning to Cork in 1992. Another female vocalist with the band is Bríd McKenna, whose amazing voice has been heard in Hong Kong, the USA and in Holland where she has lived and worked in recent years. We were often augmented by guest singers, among them Kathy Nugent who has become a regular in recent years. Kathy's career has been mainly in cabaret and shows but she has also featured with the RTÉ Concert Orchestra and was on the panel of the RTÉ TV programme *The Lyrics Board*. I get to sing a few songs over the weekend but our featured male singer is Ronnie Costley who likes to explore the song books of Neil Diamond, Frank Sinatra and Nat King Cole. Mick Lynch, who is in the Band of the Southern Command joins us on sax, clarinet and flute. A superb musician, he has been on the Cork jazz scene for as long as I can remember. So too is Michael O'Brien, who has played with all the legendary Cork jazz groups including The Second City Orchestra, and Harry and Friends. Michael led his own band at the Cork Festival for many years, attracting capacity attendances at his sessions in the Metropole Hotel. Gerry Walsh is a veteran of the Regal and Michael O'Callaghan showbands, and other members of our motley crew include bassist George Hart and Australian-born guitarist Ian Date who once accompanied Sarah Vaughan on her tour 'Down Under'. We all got together a few years ago to record a live CD which is introduced by Paddy Cole and includes 19 tracks which give a true flavour of Actons over the October Bank Holiday weekend.

The 'Fringe' emerged from the early days of the Cork Jazz Festival when visiting musicians would hop down to Kinsale for the seafood and the relaxed seaside atmosphere. Inevitably jam sessions emerged and before long, a satellite event began to develop in Actons Hotel. Thanks to the great efforts of Billy Crosbie and some valuable publicity in 'De Paper', the 'Fringe' grew and is today a well established and integral part of the Cork Festival. Cork is known internationally as 'The Friendly Jazz Festival' but Kinsale goes one step further. The sessions are very relaxed and the emphasis is on Dixieland and swing. Visiting stars often come down for a 'blow' and nobody was surprised over the years when the likes of Kenny Ball or Acker Bilk strolled up to the stage. These musicians play 'my kind of jazz'. I went to see Kenny Ball and his band on one occasion in Blackpool. He plays tight arrangements with distinctive harmonies and he had a string of hits including *Midnight in Moscow*. Acker Bilk also had a trademark clarinet sound which became world famous when he recorded the international hit *Stranger on the Shore*. We met up at a VATS Hall of Fame event in the Country Club Portmarnock in 1975 and I remember with fondness his ready wit and banter.

My most memorable jazz gig, however, was when I played with Maynard Ferguson in the Camelot Hotel in Raheny in the early 1970s. At that time the great Canadian trumpeter was living in Manchester, having taught for several years in India. Before that of course, he had played with Stan Kenton and led his own band in the USA. For the two Dublin gigs, he agreed to play with a band of local musicians which was put together by Noel Kelehan who asked Roger McGuinness to take the baritone seat. Roger and I were the only two baritone players on the Dublin circuit at that time and he very kindly offered me the seat for the second night. I had just one rehearsal with the band but I had no problem reading the score. I remember it as a very exciting and musically stimulating session with some outstanding arrangements and Ferguson's trademark high register trumpet soaring above the reeds and rhythm sections.

After the gig we had a chance to chat to the great man and Shay Nolan, himself a fine trumpet player, was naturally curious about how Maynard achieved those soaring high notes while remaining perfectly in tune.

'I just blow, man,' was the short reply.

'JUST BLOW,' Shay exploded, 'You do in your bollix.'

It was one of those nights.

Pat Egan ...
Managing the Comeback

When I was writing about the Beat
Groups scene in *New Spotlight*
magazine back in the 1960s, I was
aware of Sonny Knowles as a singer
with The Pacific Showband and over
the years I knew him to be one of the
most successful cabaret performers
in Ireland. It often struck me at the
time that Sonny could have also
been a very big cabaret star in
Britain, had he chosen to work there.

Over the years I watched his
career unfold and enjoyed listening to his albums, which featured very
fine arrangements of well chosen songs performed impeccably with a
keen appreciation for the lyrics and nuances of the melodies. I was
then involved in record retailing and I know that a Sonny Knowles LP
would simply walk off the shelves.

After he had recovered from two encounters with serious illness,
we met one evening in the National Concert Hall and I suggested to
him that his career could run to another phase in which he would
perform in large concert venues rather than the pubs and cabaret
rooms which he had made his home for three decades. He agreed to
sing in a comeback concert in the same National Concert Hall and was
joined by Tony Kenny and some musicians with whom he had a long
association. The event was a huge success. We sold out on two
successive nights and his fans really appreciated hearing him sing
again.

To mark the comeback, Paul O'Reilly of Dolphin Records agreed to release a CD of some of Sonny's best recordings. Ronan Collins helped Sonny to select what they considered his best songs. The CD went Platinum, selling more than 15,000 copies. A second CD of *Love Songs* followed, which also sold very well.

Since then I have been delighted to be associated with Sonny who has performed to full houses in prestige venues such as the Cork Opera House and the University of Limerick Concert Hall as well as the National Concert Hall. He is a total professional who loves to perform and is, in turn, much loved by his large army of fans.

Sonny ranks with people like Ronnie Drew and David Norris as a 'quintessential Dubliner' and has entertained several generations of people in his native city and further afield. Indeed wherever people love to chill out and relax with a good song, Sonny is the man to deliver it in style.

CHAPTER 10

Radio Days

The radio has always been part of my life. In our first home in Chancery Lane, we had an old wireless that was on all day and every evening playing music from the BBC and Radio Éireann. It was the same in Drimnagh, where I first became fascinated with the music of the big swing bands. The BBC played music most of the day including a half hour called *Music While You Work* featuring Victor Sylvester and His Orchestra, probably the best strict tempo dance band of them all. They toured Ireland on several occasions and were much loved by ballroom dancers for their precise playing of foxtrots, quick steps and old time waltzes. It was on BBC Radio that I also first heard the music of Ted Heath, Joe Loss, Geraldo and the other big bands of the era and on Sunday nights we would tune into *Grand Hotel*, a programme of light classical music featuring The

Palm Court Orchestra, conducted over the years by Albert Sandler, Tom Jenkins, Max Jaffa and Reginald Leopold. The programme was originally broadcast from the Grand Hotel, Eastbourne but later also from other venues and had an amazing run from 1943 to 1973 with a special celebratory revival in 1995. Another long-running favourite was *Desert Island Discs* in which personalities from the worlds of sport, politics, entertainment, business, etc. are invited to select their favourite pieces of music and talk about their lives. Roy Plomley, who presented the show from 1942 until his death in 1985, invited more than 2,000 guests to be imaginary 'castaways'. He was succeeded in turn by Michael Parkinson, Sue Lawley and Kirsty Young who presented her first show in 2006. Other memorable BBC radio shows that we enjoyed included *Midday Music Hall, Henry Hall's Guest Night, Housewives' Choice, Sing Something Simple, Record Roundup, Melody Hour* and shows from the Tower Ballroom in Blackpool, featuring the organist Sandy McPherson whose real name was Roderick Hallowell.

Radio Éireann was also a wonderful source of music and entertainment as well as being an education for an aspiring young musician like myself. We would listen to Peggy Dell play the piano and sing with her unusual and very attractive husky voice, Albert Healy who accompanied all the great crooners of the day, the Radio Éireann Light Orchestra conducted by people like Dermot O'Hara, and music programmes presented by Joe Linnane and Eric Bowden. The sponsored programmes were also a unique feature of the Radio Éireann schedule and provided a platform for many Irish musicians of the time. Waltons featured Irish music as did Gael Linn while Bird's, Donnelly's, Imco, Prescott's, Glen Abbey and others helped launch both Irish musicians and presenters such as Gay Byrne,

Terry Wogan and Val Doonican on their careers. Val Doonican liked to recall that his first hit was a jingle for Donnelly's skinless sausages that contained the immortal lines:

'To be true they're the talk of the nation
They are something excitingly new
They are truly a skinless sensation
And Donnelly's make them for you'

Other jingles that are still etched in my mind (and probably the minds of many people of my generation) include:

'Boom, boom, boom, boom
Esso Blue'

and

'A cleaning and a pressing and a drying that's true
We keep cleaning and a pressing 'til we make it like new
Imco Cleaners are the best, and if you doubt that's true
There's an Imco Clean and Pressing for You'

Those with romantic and other personal issues could get advice from Frankie Byrne on the Jacob's programmes, which invariably featured the music of her hero Frank Sinatra. At the end of each day, families all over Ireland would tune into the Irish Hospitals Sweepstakes programme presented by Bart Bastable and Ian Priestly Mitchell.

My own first radio shows were with *The Light Orchestra* when I was given a seat if the orchestra was augmented for big band music or to accompany a star singer. I was also in the orchestra for a series called *Sound of the Light* and I still remember the excitement of the sound created by a full orchestra of strings, woodwind, reeds, brass and percussion. To be sitting in the middle of such a large group of talented musicians and to watch and hear them play note perfect after a single rehearsal was an awesome experience for a young sax player learning his trade.

My first solo spot as a singer was as a guest on some of these radio shows and again it was a great experience and pleasure to be backed by a full orchestra. Gay Byrne then gave me a spot on his radio show in which I would chat to him and sing a song, while presenters such as Val Joyce, Maxi, Brendan Balfe and especially Ronan Collins frequently featured my records on their shows. All this led to an invitation to present my own radio programme which was called *Sonny Sunday*, which involved me singing and introducing guests such as Kathy Nugent or Des Smyth. The programme went out on a Sunday afternoon, which was not exactly a prime time spot but it proved to be very popular and ran for 13 weeks.

I knew nothing at all about my most memorable radio show of all until the very last minute. It was coming up to my 60th birthday and Joe Duffy was then a reporter on the *Gay Byrne Radio Show*. He came up with the idea of celebrating my Big Day by having a party with 60 women from Perrystown who would arrive at our house and 'jump on me' in bed. He discussed the idea with Sheila, who fortunately put him off the bedroom scene, but agreed to co-operate in a 'surprise party' about which I would know nothing until it actually happened. In the weeks before the event, Sheila seemed to be taking a number of confidential phone calls and when I would enquire about who was on the phone she would say something like, 'Oh, that was the girl from Hickeys about the new carpet.' In fact it was Joe Duffy who was trying to discover when I would be out of the house so that he could meet up with Sheila and take background notes. When he finally arrived, I was out somewhere and he sat down at our kitchen table. During the note-taking, a knock came to the door and Joe, thinking it was me returning ahead of schedule, had to hide in the kitchen cupboard until the identity of the caller was discovered.

Joe put his plan together and Sheila was given strict instructions that I was not to listen to RTÉ radio on the morning of my birthday. This proved to be difficult to achieve as I always have the radio on in the mornings. Geraldine, my daughter, had come over from Kent for my birthday and had brought along a friend called Penny, who was a London policewoman. She must have been a top class interrogator because they both kept me talking throughout the entire morning so that I never got around to switching on the radio.

Eventually the doorbell rang and when I answered it, I was confronted by Joe and an open-top bus crammed with 60 ladies who had been assembled by Joe with the help of Nancy Lynch, our local public relations person and dynamic worker for the community. I was escorted onto the bus and as we drove around Muckross Park, the double decker managed to pull down a few phone lines.

With Joe relaying a commentary to the nation, we drove into the city centre and stopped outside Clerys, where I was greeted by some of my best friends from the music world including Paddy Cole, Noel V. Ginnity, Eileen Reid, Earl Gill, Sil Fox, Des Smyth and several others. A cake was produced from Ann's Hot Bread Shop in Henry Street and we all joined in an impromptu concert before going off to breakfast in Clerys Restaurant. Later we returned to Crumlin in the bus and ended off my best ever birthday with a party in the Submarine Bar. Life does not get better than that and I am eternally grateful to Gay Byrne, Joe Duffy, Sheila and everybody else who created such a splendid surprise.

Irish listeners were familiar with pirate radio for generations. Back in the Forties and Fifties, a number of small amateur stations broadcast locally without much interference from the authorities, largely because they were of poor quality and attracted few listeners. Radio Luxembourg was also a 'pirate' in the sense that it broadcast to the UK and Ireland from a base in the Duchy of Luxembourg and was therefore not under the jurisdiction of the Irish or British broadcasting regulators. Broadcasting on '108 on the Medium Wave', the station was a pioneer in developing a young audience with a series of pop music programmes featuring all the hit songs of the day. Its weekly *Top 20* was a hugely influential programme in terms of promoting an artist and the size of its audience. Its ratings were initially based on sales of sheet music but this later became record sales. The style and content of Radio Luxembourg was largely based on the American Forces Network (AFN) station, which had been broadcast throughout Europe since the days of the Second World War and was a source of jazz music which influenced many of Europe's legendary jazz musicians of the 1950s.

The first high-profile pirate radio station, however, was Radio Caroline which began transmitting in 1964 from a Dutch passenger ferry anchored off the East Coast of England. Its managing director was Ronan O'Rahilly, a colourful character who claimed that he had named the station after Caroline Kennedy, daughter of JFK. This story later proved to be just a publicity stunt but Radio Caroline flourished for about five years, during which it attracted a growing volume of advertising and a huge and young audience from both Britain and Ireland. Changes in UK law eventually led to its collapse but the name is still retained by a licensed commercial radio station in Britain.

A group of ex-Radio Caroline people including Chris Carey and Robbie Robinson (aka Robbie Dale) arrived in Ireland in 1980 to launch a new pirate radio station which would operate at the fringes of the then broadcasting laws. Before the venture went on air however the group divided, with Robbie Robinson launching Sunshine Radio and Chris Carey launching Radio Nova. They were not the first pirate radio stations in the country – Radio Dublin had been broadcasting since 1966 and both Radio Melinda and Alternative Radio Dublin (ARD) had a short life in the Seventies. Nova and Sunshine were, however, by far the most professional pirate stations of their era – or indeed any other. Sunshine broadcast from a studio at the Sands Hotel in Portmarnock and Nova's base was in Herbert Place. Both operated openly with commercial offices, presenters broadcasting under their own names and published telephone numbers and were more or less ignored by the authorities. They attracted a young audience and high volumes of advertising and were a serious challenge to the dominant position of RTÉ radio.

Around this time I met up with Danny Hughes, who had operated beat clubs in Dublin and Limerick in the Sixties and who was an active impresario. He ran a weekly tea dance at Jurys Hotel in Ballsbridge and I did a regular spot there for more than two years with singer Rose Tynan. Around that time Danny was involved in setting up a pirate radio station called Radio Leinster and he asked me to present a weekly music programme. At that time I had an ambition to develop my career into radio presentation and this appeared to be a good opportunity to get some valuable experience. The studio was located in the garage of a bungalow behind Lamb Doyle's in the Dublin Mountains and it was populated by a motley crew of eager, young broadcasters, including Gavin Duffy, several of whom later developed careers in mainstream broadcasting. The programme content was closer to that of RTÉ Radio One than a pop station and included specialist current affairs programmes as well as slots for jazz, big bands, music from the movies, classical music and a business programme called Working Breakfast, which was presented by Frank Corr who is working with me on this book. The station achieved some notoriety when Gavin Duffy interviewed Seán Mac Stíofáin who was banned from RTÉ and received a call from the Special Branch as a result. What it had in terms of creativity, enthusiasm and style, it lacked in commercial expertise and the station eventually folded due to lack of revenue. My days at Radio Leinster provided me with valuable experience in radio presentation and in communicating with an audience on air. It also gave me an opportunity to play requests for my fans and to promote my own recordings. On the other hand, it probably ended my days as an RTÉ radio presenter as the national broadcaster did not take kindly to singers who had programmes on rival pirate stations.

I did, however, become a presenter on RTÉ Television when I became front man on my own TV show. It emerged as a result of some work I did with VATS, the Variety Artists' Trust Society, which looks after retired and infirm actors, musicians and technicians, visiting them regularly, organising Christmas hampers and outings. It was a tribute show for Peggy Dell – that wonderful pianist and singer who performed well into her Eighties. My brother Harry had played in her band and I was one of her greatest admirers. I was MC at the show and sang a few songs and later in Madigan's Pub in Donnybrook (known to RTÉ staff as 'Studio Five'), Tom McGrath said he had an idea of creating a show called *Cabaret* which would feature some of the top performers of the day. He invited me to present the show and I was delighted to accept, although I had never done anything like that on television. Typically I called on my friends in the business and we put together a series of shows in which I would sing a few numbers, introduce my guests, have a chat with them, get them to do their spot and maybe do a duet with them before rounding off the programme. We attracted all the big names in cabaret, including comedians Al Bannon and Sil Fox and singers like Dickie Rock and the great Joe Dolan who was the biggest cabaret act in Ireland for more than three decades. I was a great admirer of Joe who was the consummate showman and a magnificent singer. He had a charismatic personality, which was unmatched by any Irish performer I knew and if you put him on in the biggest hall in Ireland in the middle of nowhere, he would fill it to the rafters. I loved his soaring voice, his musicianship and his ability to find songs that he could make his own. I was in the same business as Joe but I knew that I could never match his pulling power or ability to reach out to his audience. He was always a good friend and sent me front row tickets to any show he did in Dublin. Sheila and I always went along and enjoyed the shows as much as any of his myriad fans. When Joe died, his road manager sent me two of the tickets I had used to see one of his concerts and they remain among my most treasured souvenirs of a great entertainer.

Appearing on television before a live audience was quite a nerve-wracking experience but by the time the cameras rolled we were usually well prepared. Tom McGrath had assembled a first class band for the show which included Bill Whelan, a talented musician from Limerick who worked with Planxty in its early days and composed the music for *Riverdance* among a varied output of classical, traditional and popular music. Earl Gill was also in the lineup as were Eamon Campbell (who later joined The Dubliners), Des Reynolds on drums, John Curran, Jack Beale and Eddie Tighe. Our pre-show preparations began with a day when we would meet up with our guest for the week and discuss the content. Earl would run over the music and allocate arrangements to members of the band, while I would chat with the guest about what we would talk about on the show. At a second rehearsal, the arrangements would be completed and we would run over the music content with the guest while I would finalise the script. This would set us up for the live recording on a studio set that resembled a cabaret room complete with tables for the guests. It was a lovely show which attracted good ratings and I was more than happy with my first experience as a TV presenter.

My next TV spot was on *Live at Three*, which was presented by Thelma Mansfield. During the show I would sing a few numbers with a piano accompaniment. After one show, Joe McCormack, the producer, asked me if I would do an interview. 'No problem,' I replied. 'Who will be interviewing me?'

'Nobody,' replied Joe. 'It's you who will be conducting the interview.'

'But I don't know how to interview people,' I protested.

'Just chat to them,' said Joe.

And so it was that I began interviewing guests one day a week on *Live at Three*. Luckily they were mainly friends of mine so there was no great pressure. Usually I would meet them before the show and ask, 'What would you like me to ask you?' This agreed, they would come onto the set after my spot and I would chat to them briefly before they did their own spot. It was not exactly *Prime Time* but it was nevertheless a new departure for me and more valuable experience in the world of communications. It also worked very well. After a few shows, just about everybody in showbusiness wanted to be interviewed by Sonny on *Live at Three*.

My biggest TV audience however was in the UK – and they saw me for only about a minute. *Ballykissangel* was a series conceived by the BBC and filmed in Avoca and Enniskerry. It ran for five seasons between 1996 and 2001 and featured a largely Irish cast that included Dervla Kirwan, Tony Doyle, Bosco Hogan, Birdy Sweeney, Stephen Brennan, Niall Tobin, Áine Ní Mhuirí, Tina Kellegher, Deirdre Donnelly, Colin Farrell, Don Wycherley, Catherine Cusack, Joe Savino, Marion O'Dwyer, Mick Lally and Victoria Smurfit.

In one episode, the character played by Jim Norton has returned to Ballykissangel and has fallen for the local shop assistant. They go for a walk and pass a poster advertising 'An Evening with Sonny Knowles'. They decide to go along and there is a scene in which I am given one line of dialogue and then sing a few bars of a song called *Sure She's Irish*.

The show had a huge following in Britain with thousands of tourists travelling over to Wicklow to visit Avoca. It was also sold by the BBC to stations around the world. By this time, our children had moved to Australia and one evening we got a phone call from an excited daughter who yelled down the line, 'Hey Dad – you're famous in Australia. You are on *Ballykissangel*.'

So much for stardom.

Jim Farley ...
'Sax Brother'

The saxophone has been the bond between Sonny Knowles and myself for close on 50 years. We began playing together with The Earl Gill Band in the Palm Court Ballroom around 1960 – and we are still making music together today.

We first sat together in the reed section of an Earl Gill Band at the premiere of the film *Darby O'Gill and the Little People* at the Shelbourne Hotel in 1959. Earl had been asked to form a band for the occasion and since then we have referred to him as 'Darby'.

When Sonny joined The Palm Court Band, he did not sing at the beginning but on one occasion when our vocalist Dick Dorney felt that he could not master a current pop song, Sonny put up his hand and said, 'I'll have a go at that.'

The rest, as they say, is history.

When Earl Gill took his band to the USA to tour with Ruby Murray, both Sonny and I were included. We had a fabulous time in New York, where some of the great jazz legends played regularly in small clubs. We would just pop around the corner after a gig and walk into a session featuring some jazz legend. At our gigs, Sonny would rarely play solos but we often did saxophone duets together, recreating the sound of Billy Vaughan.

The Earl Gill Band played mostly in Dublin but occasionally we went 'on tour' to Galway or Waterford. Some serious drinking would be

148

undertaken along the return route and the band would be in some state when we finally arrived back to the Shelbourne. Sonny, however, managed somehow to stay sober on these occasions. On one memorable trip to Waterford, Terry (my wife), Sheila, Sonny and I travelled in an old banger of a car that kept overheating. We were forced to stop at the Red Cow and then every few miles until we finally reached our destination.

After playing together for some years, we went our separate ways – Sonny to The Pacific Showband and me to form the 13-piece Jim Farley Big Band, which included the great trumpet player Joe McIntyre, Neil McMahon and singers Terry Mahon and Danny Pierce. Our manager was the equally legendary Nelius O'Connell.

Before long, however, we were back together again. The showbands had given way to cabaret and Sonny was carving out a new career as a cabaret artist and MC. He presided over the shows at the Drake Inn in Finglas and often invited me to join him in bands that would accompany stars like Matt Munro and Max Bygraves. This was the heyday of cabaret in Dublin with venues like the Drake Inn, the Tudor Room, the Braemor Room and later the Chariot Inn in Ranelagh and the Fiesta Club in Pearse Street. All the big stars came to Dublin to head the bill, often for a week, and in the process provided plenty of work for musicians. Sonny was the Irish star on this scene and we had some great times together.

Sonny began his career as a sax and clarinet player and always retained his interest in playing music. Indeed he still plays at the annual Kinsale Fringe Jazz Festival. We played regularly in the big band at 'The Fed', in the Irish Federation of Musicians Hall, where musicians gathered on Tuesdays for a jam session. Although Sonny was then best known to the public as a singer, he was recognised by fellow musicians as a fine sax player and an excellent reader of music. After playing alto in his early years, he switched to baritone sax and was one of the few musicians on the Dublin scene who specialised in this instrument.

We played one memorable jazz concert together in Dublin when we were in a band headed by the great Maynard Ferguson at the Camelot Hotel. Jack Bayle organised the band and had Roger McGuinness on baritone for the first concert and Sonny for the second. It was quite an experience.

While our careers took different directions over the years – Sonny in cabaret and me in bands like Daddy Cool and Lollipops – we have remained very close friends. It is therefore a great pleasure for me to be in his backing band since his comeback. He just walks on stage at the Cork Opera House, the Helix or the National Concert Hall and the audience responds immediately. Who else would appear at these venues and have fans walking up to the stage and handing him notes and requests? He always responds, indicating with his famous finger signals, that he is about to break from his present medley into some tune that has just been requested.

I think I now know the real 'Daddy Cool'.

It is my friend Sonny.

CHAPTER 11

Cancer

Health, they say, is wealth and from that point of view I was always a wealthy man. Even though my father died from pneumonia when I was only seven years of age, I seemed to inherit healthy genes and sailed through life with only the occasional cough or cold. Not that I was particularly health-conscious. The fact is that I took my good health for granted and got on with life. I was never a smoker and while I enjoyed the occasional brandy and port, I was not a heavy drinker, even in the days when I was on the road with the showbands and spent a lot of time in the company of heavy-drinking colleagues. Neither did I take a lot of exercise. As soon as I became a professional musician in my early twenties, I gave up hiking and biking with An Óige and my boxing days also ended. My only real exercise was pottering around in the garden and taking the occasional stroll with Sheila, although I would also swim in the hotel pool when we were on tour. I was always a nifty swimmer and when the children were young, I loved to show off by doing somersaults off the top diving board. During one such display, I tore a shoulder muscle and was in agony for the next nine weeks. I went to every hospital and doctor I could find and finally to an acupuncturist before the muscle healed. So much for showboating.

Looking back over the years, I could say that I was a passive smoker, spending every working night in smoke-filled dance halls, pubs and cabaret rooms, and that could not have been healthy. Indeed it is amazing that, until fairly recent times, we tolerated smoking in all kinds of enclosed spaces and were happy to expose those who worked there to a continuous haze of dangerous tobacco fumes.

My eating habits would also be frowned upon by any nutritionist. On the road with the showbands, we tended to eat muck – deep fried burgers and chips and onion rings and maybe steaks and pasta, followed by creamy desserts. I was particularly fond of curry and the Bombay Restaurant in Richmond Street did the best curries in Dublin. On many a night when I finished my act somewhere down the country, I would phone the owner and ask him what time he planned to close. 'What time can you be here?' he would ask. 'I'm in Mullingar – I'll be there in two hours,' I would tell him. 'OK Sonny, we'll have your curry ready,' he would say. And he did.

What healthy food I had was cooked by Sheila who could also make a super curry with all the trimmings. Mostly she would cook good traditional meals with potatoes and vegetables, and these helped balance the junk food that I consumed on tour. Sheila is also an excellent baker, a skill she inherited from her mother Eileen who baked our wedding cake. She continues to produce tempting cakes and desserts that I have enjoyed over the years.

For more than six decades, therefore, I was a picture of good health, reasonably fit and happy to the world. So when I began to urinate a little bit more frequently than normal, I took little notice. It was only when the problem persisted and I was in and out of bed several times in a night that I became concerned. I mentioned it to Gay Byrne who gave me sound advice. 'Sonny,' he said, 'Get that checked.'

When I went to my local doctor, he was surprised to see me. 'You have not been here for a few years,' he said. 'I know, Doctor,' I replied, 'That's because I wasn't sick.' I realised then of course that I should have been to see him for regular health checkups. He sent me to Mount Carmel Hospital for tests and the result was that I was told that I had prostate cancer.

'Cancer' – it was a word I always dreaded and one that equated in my mind with a death sentence. I was shocked to the core and thought that my life was over. 'Why me?' was the question I asked myself every day.

Like many men of my generation in Ireland, I had very little knowledge about health matters and the risk of illness in middle age. I knew little or nothing about my prostate gland but I knew that if the word 'cancer' was mentioned in connection with it, then my condition was serious. In the following weeks and months, I would learn a lot more about my condition and if I had known then what I know now, my treatment could probably have commenced earlier.

What I learned is that the prostate is a small gland located underneath the bladder in men. It is shaped like a doughnut and fits around the tube (called the urethra), which carries urine out of the bladder. The prostate produces the fluid that mixes with sperm when a man ejaculates.

Prostate cancer is a very variable disease. Some tumours remain small and grow so slowly that they cause no problems and often remain undetected for decades; others are aggressive, grow quickly and become life-threatening. Many of these aggressive cases spread to the bones, where they cause severe pain.

Prostate cancer is now the most commonly diagnosed cancer in men in many western countries. The number of recorded cases has increased a lot in recent years, partly due to the use of the Prostate Specific Antigen (PSA) test, which has resulted in more cases being detected, and partly due to the fact that men are living longer. Like most cancers, prostate cancer is more common in the elderly.

The main symptoms are difficulty in passing urine, inability to urinate, passing urine often (particularly at night), weak or interrupted urine flow, pain when urinating, blood in the urine and pain in the lower back, hips and upper thighs. However all of these symptoms can also be caused by other conditions such as benign prostate enlargement.

The good news is that if prostate cancer is diagnosed early, it can be treated very successfully. However, when the cancer is advanced, it becomes very difficult to cure. So health professionals recommend that men over 50 years of age should have a regular PSA test, which can be given by the family doctor. This indicates the level of PSA in the blood and can be an indicator, but not necessarily proof of prostate cancer. I didn't know any of this before I was diagnosed but had I known, I would certainly have had the PSA test at least once every two years.

My prostate tumor was in a location which made it very difficult to remove surgically so Professor Armstrong, my oncologist, decided that I would have treatment instead at St. Luke's Hospital in Rathgar. He said that the tumor had been detected early and that everything should be alright. 'You won't die from it – you will die with it,' he said. The treatment took the form of 34 sessions of radiotherapy, which uses high energy radiation to kill the cancer cells. The objective was to shrink and eventually to destroy the tumor.

When I was told that I had cancer, Sheila and I were faced with the dilemma of whether or not we should tell our children who were living in Australia. We did not want to alarm them into coming all the way to Ireland when we could probably wait for a successful outcome of the treatment and then tell them that I was in good health once again. With hindsight, this was a big mistake and the wrong thing to do. It meant that for more than six months, we had to keep my illness a secret shared only by Sheila and myself. We could not mention it to family or friends, for fear that the news would get back to the children. I tried to act normally during the treatment. I kept working here in Ireland, putting a brave face on my illness, and even went on tour to America. I was taking medication called Maalox for stomach pains and Sheila would slip them to me when needed. We both felt under terrible stress however, having to pretend to everybody that we were in good spirits while sharing the secret of my cancer between us. The treatment tended to make me tired and I would take frequent naps, joking to people that I must be getting old. I also experienced bouts of depression and would often slip off with Sheila during the American tour for a walk and a little cry.

We lived with this secret throughout my treatment, which proved to be highly successful. The tumor shrank and disappeared leaving only some scar tissue. I had checkups every three months for a while before I was given a clean bill of health. With radiotherapy I did not experience any hair loss and only relatively minor side-effects so I could keep on working without anybody knowing but the stress of keeping my illness a secret from the children took its toll.

Eventually of course, we had to tell the family and we prepared by planning a visit to Australia to see them. When we got there Sheila said: 'Here's Dad – and he's fine.'

'And why not?' they asked.

Then of course the whole story came out and understandably our children were shocked and angry that they had not been told. In truth, all hell broke out. I know that if it was my own father who was ill, I would have been shocked and angry too. We explained as best we could but we both knew that we had taken a wrong decision, which we had to live with. We promised our children that if anything similar was to happen in the future, they would be informed immediately. Little did we know that we would have more bad news for them within a few years. Eventually of course, the anger subsided and the great tide of love which has always been within our family circle washed over the hurt and cured it.

Later on I spoke about the episode on the Gay Byrne radio programme and it sparked an enormous response. People called the show to say that they had kept dark secrets rather than get health conditions checked and others said that men are slow to go to the doctor while women are the ones who go to hospitals with their children and are therefore more accustomed to looking after their health.

It was a traumatic time for both of us and indeed for our family but I believe that it taught me two valuable lessons. The first is the advantage of going regularly to the doctor for a health check, which is likely to detect any serious illness at a very early stage. The second, of course, is the folly of keeping secrets, particularly from your own family.

The next five years were perfect. I returned to good health and my career blossomed with plenty of work available in Ireland and America. As the Celtic Tiger roared along, people were enjoying themselves, going out in the evenings to dine and dance and be entertained. The corporate sector was booming and companies were only too happy to entertain their clients. I was only too happy to be part of that scene, singing my songs, enjoying the music and the company and a relaxed family life with Sheila. We went on frequent holidays to Spain, visited our children in Australia regularly and chilled out in our holiday home in Co. Wexford. All thoughts of illness in general, and cancer in particular, faded away and cancer became just a distant memory.

Then it returned – with a vengeance.

The first hint that all was not well was when I sang at a charity event in Kilmuckridge in aid of the local Community Hall. The place was packed in the middle of Summer and I felt very warm in my white showbiz suit complete with waistcoat. I had removed my jacket when a friend said that the waistcoat was too big for me and maybe I should tighten it a bit. It was only then that I realised that it fitted me perfectly until then and that I must have been losing weight without knowing it. Later in the evening, I had a tummy pain but put it down to a bug or virus. We had booked a holiday in Tunisia and were due to fly out on the following day. We thought that the tummy problem would pass in a few days and decided that we would not cancel the trip.

That was a mistake.

Tunisia in North Africa is a very beautiful country with miles of white sandy beaches and modern luxury hotels. We settled into our hotel, just on the beach, but very soon I realised that all was not well. The tummy pains got worse and I could literally watch my flesh fall away as I lost weight very rapidly. To make matters worse, we were on a package holiday and there was no way we could get a flight back to Ireland before our holiday ended. So for two weeks Sheila and I remained in the hotel, getting increasingly worried about my condition. I could not eat and slept only fitfully and Sheila, I know, was sick with worry.

When we finally got back to Dublin, I dashed to see our family GP, Dr. Agina, who immediately sent me to St. James's Hospital for a scope. When I returned there a few days later for the result, the nurse said: 'Nice to see you, Mr. Knowles. We have a bed ready for you.'

'Jesus,' I thought. 'For what?' and tears welled up again at the very thought of another serious illness.

Sheila came to the hospital with me. A nurse took her aside and put her arms around her shoulders. 'Don't upset yourself,' she said gently, 'but we are not ruling out cancer.'

It was then that I met Professor John Reynolds, the man who saved my life. He sent me first of all to the Blackrock Clinic and then to the Mater Hospital for tests and when he was fully satisfied, he told me that I had a malignant tumor in my oesophagus.

Cancer again.

The oesophagus, which translates from the Latin into 'entrance for eating' is also known as the gullet. It is an organ which consists of a 25-30 centimetre muscular tube through which food passes from the mouth to the stomach. It is divided into cervical, thoracic and abdominal parts. Due to the fact that the oesophagus lacks a mucus lining, like that of the stomach, it can get irritated by stomach acid.

Tumors can develop in the oesophagus and they usually lead to a difficulty in swallowing, pain and weight loss. Small and localised tumors can be removed by surgery but larger tumors can only be treated with chemotherapy and radiotherapy.

Luckily my tumor was at a stage where it was possible to remove it by surgery. It would be a delicate and complex operation but Professor Reynolds was confident that it would be successful and his confidence was most reassuring to me. He took great care in preparing for the operation and spoke in detail to Sheila about my background. When he discovered that I made my living from singing, he said that he would be particularly careful about preserving the integrity of my vocal chords so that when I recovered I could continue singing. At that stage my only thoughts were about survival but I was nevertheless very appreciative of his concern for my career.

Jenny Moore is a saint. She is specialist clinical nurse to Professor Reynolds and she played a most important role in preparing Sheila and myself for the surgery which lay ahead. She drew diagrams and models and explained every aspect of the procedure in great detail, step by step. She explained that the tumor was midway down the oesophagus, that it had been detected at an early stage and that the chances of successful surgery were very high. The only concerns of the medical team related to my age and my ability to survive what was a major operation. It involved the collapsing of my lung, breaking through ribs, removing the tumor and part of my stomach. Every aspect of the procedure was explained to us in advance and the knowledge and honesty of the team gave us hope and confidence because we knew that we were in the best of hands.

This time, of course, we told the family immediately and they were a source of tremendous support. The operation was originally set for a Friday but a minor problem at the hospital resulted in a postponement to the following Monday. I went home for the weekend but found it impossible to relax. Despite all the assurances from the medical team, I was scared that this would be the end of my life.

When it finally came to going to the theatre for the operation, I felt curiously relaxed – probably because I was drugged with painkillers and relaxants. Professor Reynolds greeted me and told me that everything would be alright – and I believed him totally.

And he was right.

The surgery, while very difficult and complex, was a complete success. Professor Reynolds succeeded brilliantly in removing the entire tumor without any spread of the cancer and the only real side-effect was that my stomach was a lot smaller than it had been prior to the surgery – which, all told, might not be a bad thing.

Recovery was a slow but steady process. I was of course weak after the surgery and got tired very quickly. I also had difficulty eating and could only consume liquids or liquidised foods for several months. I remember a note on my hospital room door which said 'Soft Foods Only'. Sheila was a veritable 'Florence Nightingale' as my nurse. She prepared foods that I could eat, liquidised them and fed me small amounts whenever I needed to eat. I was 13 stone 7lbs before I became ill and I emerged as a 9 stone 7lb weakling. I needed a lot of care and attention to build myself back and Sheila was there for me every hour of the day and night. Gradually I began to walk a little, first around the house and then in the garden and finally around our estate.

Slowly I began to eat again – tiny amounts at first and then a little more. Because my stomach is only about half of its former size, however, I will always have to eat little and often. When I was recovering in hospital, I had a few sessions with a dietitian who worked out an eating plan which I was supposed to follow. It was based on eating very small amounts of food at short intervals. At first I only took soup and bread and I would usually be cranky if Sheila tried to get me to eat solid food. One day she tried to get me to eat some chicken but I said that I couldn't handle it. A little later she gave me soup, which I happily consumed. Several cups of soup later, she told me that I had consumed all the chicken which she had liquidised. After that I took my nutrition a bit more seriously.

Today my eating remains restricted but I enjoy porridge or a boiled egg in the morning and small meals maybe four or five times a day. I am also very partial to chocolate and ice cream. When we go out to eat with friends, I have to take small portions. Usually I have a quiet word with the waiter and mention 'surgery'. They generally understand and I get the portion I want.

I can't pretend that I am a good patient. In fact I hate being sick or infirm and I can be a cranky bastard at times. But Sheila has taken it all in her stride and has nurtured me back to good health again.

No greater love.

She even took radio in her stride. After the operation, Joe Duffy asked me to go on radio to talk about my illness and answer questions from listeners. I was not really up to it so I suggested that my daughter Geraldine, who was over from Australia, might do it instead. Joe thought that Sheila would be ideal and she agreed to go on the show. She did so magnificently, talking openly and honestly about the whole trauma, never hesitating or stuttering, and answering questions from listeners for a full hour. It helped, I suppose, that she knew some of the people who rang in and she was in fact chatting to friends on national radio. But it was an electrifying programme of which Sheila was the star.

As time progresses I am getting stronger and more active. Sheila and I often go to Bray (where I once played in brass bands on the seafront) for a walk on the prom and a little bit up Bray Head. I am probably getting more exercise now than in my showband days.

Since the operation we have gone on holiday to Spain and other places but the highlight was visiting the family once again in Australia and showing them that I had beaten cancer once more. We had a wonderful four month holiday, which became a most happy family reunion.

None of this would have been possible were it not for the commitment, professionalism and amazing skill of Professor John Reynolds. From the moment of diagnosis until the final checkup, he was kind, considerate, honest and above all, confident of success. We have become close friends and I am privileged to support some fundraising events for oesophageal cancer in which he is involved. I have also spoken about my illness to cancer support groups and in media interviews so that I can offer encouragement and hope to the thousands of people whose lives are utterly changed by the disease.

My experiences have proven, not once, but twice, that there IS life after cancer, that it can be tackled and overcome and that even in the most dire cases, there is hope.

I have come to realise that the best way of combating cancer is through regular screening and prevention. Smoking, for instance, seriously raises the risk of developing cancer and that applies equally to passive smoking. Early detection is also vital and I would urge men in particular to go to their GP for regular health checks including the PSA prostate test.

Cancer remains a serious, life-threatening disease but spectacular progress has been made in its treatment in recent times and many cancers can now be effectively cured or restrained.

I hope that my experience will give hope and courage to cancer patients everywhere.

Professor John Reynolds Journey to a Happy End

Cancer surgeons, oncologists, and specialist cancer nurses have the great privilege in their professional lives of meeting and helping patients and their families who are faced with the trauma of a cancer diagnosis. In my position as a cancer surgeon I am constantly humbled and in awe of wonderful people, and often remarkable loved ones, who are faced with a diagnosis and treatment that presents major physical and emotional challenges. The greatest satisfaction comes from taking a patient safely through complex surgery or other treatments, achieving a cure where it is possible, and witnessing a recovery of whatever it is that defines quality of life for the patient.

It was my privilege to meet Sonny and Sheila and care for him following his diagnosis with oesophageal cancer. He had done the right thing by seeking help as soon as he felt things were not quite right. He also had good fortune on his side, others who do the same sometimes have a less optimistic outlook, and we all need that indefinable element of luck if diagnosed with cancer. His experience with prostate cancer made him understand that cancer can be cured, and this would have helped him have confidence in the advice and encouragement he received from me, Jenny Moore and other members of the multidisciplinary team. He tells his experience like it is, major cancer surgery is tough, particularly at his age, and he lost a lot of weight and had a poor appetite and a restricted diet for months, but bit by bit he recovered.

The principal lesson from Sonny's experience is that cancer is curable, and increasingly so. An early diagnosis is key, and seeking advice on his prostate blood test some years ago, and on new and worrisome stomach symptoms before he met me, undoubtedly helped him on both occasions. Treatments can be daunting, but they are now better and safer, the risks for example of Sonny not surviving his operation on the oesophagus would have been at least three times greater twenty years ago. Cancer for many nowadays is like a chronic condition, with more people cured and living free of cancer but worried by it's threat and perhaps dealing with the consequences of treatment, as well as many living longer with the disease in remission, and quality of life is now a hugely important dimension. Sonny eventually recovered his zest for life and the preservation of his voice allowed him the prospect of regaining one of the most important elements of his quality of life.

On a personal note it has been a great pleasure to get to know Sonny and Sheila over these few years. They are a remarkable team and Sheila was an amazing source of strength and support during his illness, she truly nursed him back to health in the months after his operation. I was honoured when Sonny invited me to City West Hotel when he was presented with the prestigious Living Legend award. Over a thousand people attended that night, it was quite an insight for me and I could see how much he belonged to his adoring public and that performing again was like an oxygen supply that sustained him.

To me Sonny is a man of great natural humility and warmth who never took anything for granted, and is truly grateful for his gifts and his wonderful wife, family and friends. I suspect he knows every one of his legion of devoted admirers and treats every one as a friend with respect and appreciation. These qualities shone through during his illness and recovery and he has shown extraordinary appreciation of the many nurses and doctors that have looked after him. He has helped support cancer research at Trinity College and St. James's Hospital (CROSS charity) through attending and performing at fundraisers. More than anything else he has raised awareness of oesophageal and prostate cancer and of the patient journey. His narrative, as told by him here and in articles and interviews in the media, does not hide the reality and difficulty of facing cancer, but it is full of optimism and hope and I see every week in my cancer clinic the positive impact of his story. I thank Sonny for his personal friendship, for his support of cancer research, and I wish to convey deep gratitude and best wishes to him on behalf of the many patients that he has helped and for whom he continues to be a source of inspiration and hope.

Sil Fox ...
'Sharing a Laugh'

I was delighted when I was asked if I would tell of my friendship with the legendary Sonny Knowles. We first met more than 25 years ago in Wong's Restaurant on the Naas Road in Dublin. I was in a show in which he was appearing and he drove us to Pedigree Corner.

After the show, he gave me some advice – and if it wasn't for this advice I would be a big star to-day (Ha! Ha!). From then on, our paths crossed frequently as we shared the bill in venues like the Drake Inn, the Chariot in Ranelagh, Biddy Mulligan's, the Wexford Inn, The Braemor Room, Clare Manor or the Tudor Room. It is sad to realise that all of these fine venues have disappeared. We had great times in cabaret. At the end of a night Sonny would say: 'Silber' (that's what he called me), 'Let's have a Napper Tandy' (meaning a brandy) 'and then we'll Shoot the Moon', (meaning we would go home).

Our families grew up together. Gary, the 'Son of Sonny' and my son Alan played football together (they are both now in Australia) and I was in the Knowles' house when their daughter Aisling took her first steps which were straight over to me. Sheila, Sonny and myself all gave her a big cheer.

Sonny is a great fighter and overcame very serious illness. We were all sick with worry, but somehow I knew that he would come through. When he was recuperating I met up withy my good friend Roland Soper and together we persuaded Sonny to join us on a visit to the National Concert Hall. It was there that he met the great Pat Egan – and the rest is history. I was delighted to be part of Sonny's come-back shows and to see how everybody in the audience loved him.

Nobody knows Sonny's real age – but he remembers the First of the Mohicans. It is great to see that he remains so successful. I asked him recently how he is doing and he told me that the phone never stops ringing. I asked him why he doesn't get it fixed!

He is a true friend and a great entertainer.

May he go on and on.

CHAPTER **12**

Comeback

Getting well physically was a slow but steady process. Recovering my will and confidence to resume normal life was an altogether different matter. After the second bout of cancer, I was fully convinced that my career and my useful life were over. I was weak physically and eating only small amounts of food. I would not go out of the house but would spend my days and evenings just moping around, which was certainly not my style before the illness. I would watch television, listen to the radio or read a little but I had in fact become a couch potato.

Sheila was the essence of patience with me. She made my meals, looked after my every need and gently urged me to take a little exercise or get out into the fresh air. We had stopped going to our holiday home in Kilmuckridge and I was fully convinced that I would never see the place again.

While Sheila's gentle persuasion was kind and well-meaning, it was not very effective. After all, it was now 18 months since the operation and I was feeling strong and well again, although I refused to admit to myself that I was ready for a normal life. What I really needed was a good kick up the arse.

It was duly delivered by two good friends, Sil Fox, the comedian and Roland Soper, the songwriter and musician who is best known for composing Dickie Rock's Eurovision song *Come Back to Stay*. Both had been in touch regularly since my illness and were concocting plans to get me out into the real world once again. Their opportunity came when Matthew Munro was scheduled to appear at the National Concert Hall with the National Concert Orchestra. The boys knew that I had been a big fan of Matthew's father, Matt Munro whom I had met at the Drake Inn. They knew that I could be tempted to go to the concert and duly booked tickets. I was slow to accept their invitation but felt that I could not refuse two such good friends. Even an hour before they arrived to collect me, I tried to cop out but Sheila insisted that I go upstairs, put on my suit and be ready.

We duly went to the National Concert Hall, heard Matthew sing and met him afterwards for some nostalgic chat about his great father. It was then that I was introduced to a silver-haired gentleman whose opening words after we shook hands were 'Sonny – I am going to manage your comeback.'

'Well good luck to you,' was my response, 'because I am not coming back.'

Pat Egan, however, was not a man to take 'no' for an answer. We talked generally and he said that I had a big following who would warmly welcome the opportunity to hear me singing again. I told him that my voice was as good as ever but that I had been very ill and did not see how I could go back on the road.

Next day I had a call from another great friend, Ronan Collins, the RTÉ radio presenter and former showband drummer. He said that Pat Egan had told him about our conversation of the previous night and that he wanted to say to me that he had known Pat for more than 40 years and that he would 'do me no harm'. He assured me that Pat would look after me well and that I would not be overworked. Never having worked with a manager since my days in The Pacific Showband, I was apprehensive about being managed at this stage of my life. In the event, I agreed to meet up with Pat for a further chat, during which he proposed a comeback show in the National Concert Hall. I could pick my own backing musicians and guests, and the event would be widely publicised. It was, I suppose, an offer I could not refuse. After years of singing in pubs and clubs, the stage of the National Concert Hall appealed to me. It is a lovely space set into the former Aula Maxima of University College Dublin, with a handsome foyer complete with a magnificent Waterford crystal chandelier. And, of course, it has played host to some of the most outstanding musicians in the world since it first opened in 1981. It is, in a way, our own Carnegie Hall and a treasured national asset that stages more than 500 concerts and recitals every year.

I was not exactly a stranger to the stage of the NCH as I had played there on several occasions with the RTÉ orchestras. On another occasion I sang at the NCH with Michael Casey playing its magnificent concert organ. This would be my first opportunity to headline a show at the great venue. I agreed – and promptly headed off to Australia to visit our family for three months.

When I returned, the date for my comeback had been set. As he had promised, Pat Egan had booked the National Concert Hall and had begun a publicity campaign. The response was both a surprise and very heartwarming. The people who had come to the Drake Inn, Slattery's and countless other venues over the years, including hundreds who had sent me goodwill messages, wanted to hear me sing again and as a result they booked out the NCH for two successive evenings. We brought Andy O'Callaghan on board as our musical director for the evening. Andy is an accomplished musician and he helped me compile a set list for the concert. This was something I did earlier in my career but as time went on, I developed such a close rapport with my backing musicians that the show would just flow along without us ever having a list of songs. The National Concert Hall was a more formal affair however and Andy did new arrangements of the songs I was to sing. Ronan Collins put a band together which included some of my close musical friends and he played drums himself. I was able to return a compliment to my good friend Tony Kenny by inviting him to guest, just as he had invited me to guest on his shows over the years and Sil Fox came along to put everyone in the best of humour.

In the run-up to the show, Pat Egan introduced me to Paul O'Reilly of Dolphin Records, who had the idea of releasing a compilation CD of my recordings. Over the years I had recorded more than 50 tracks which appeared on LPs. I would like to say that they were all smash hits – but the opposite is probably true. I have often told friends that I could not give them away free with petrol. The LPs represented my musical output over most of my career and many of the tracks had very fine arrangements. Paul O'Reilly took them away, had a listen and asked Ronan Collins for advice. Together they selected about 40 tracks that they liked and had them digitally remastered. The result was excellent – the sound was crisp and clear with a warm tonal quality. It was decided to release the CD, called *Sonny – The Very Best of Sonny Knowles*, to coincide with the National Concert Hall show. Thanks to the expertise of Paul and Pat and the support of good friends like Ronan, Maxi and other presenters, plus people who sent in requests, it popped up regularly on radio programmes. When I was told a few months later that the CD had 'gone Platinum', meaning that sales had topped 15,000 copies, I was gobsmacked – and truly delighted. The CD includes many of my favourite songs such as *I'll Take Care of Your Cares, No One Knows, My Child, Roses of Picardy, When the Snow is on the Roses* and *Three Good Reasons*. Dolphin followed this with a second CD called *The Love Songs Collection*, which has tracks such as *Music from Across the Way, For the Good Times, Can I Forget You, Solitaire* and *Help Me Make it Through the Night,* among others.

The NCH show was a huge success and did just what Pat Egan had promised – revived a career that I thought was over.

Shortly before the event, I had actually signed off on that career by participating in a PATS charity evening at City West Hotel, during which I was presented with a 'Living Legend' award. PATS is the Performing Artists Trust Society and is the new name for VATS, which I have already mentioned. It raises funds to help people in the entertainment industry who have fallen on hard times and I agreed to provide my services at this event without charging a fee as I had done on many occasions in the past.

On one such occasion they presented me with a 'Lifetime Achievement' award and now that I was also a 'Living Legend',

I got the feeling that my career might be heading towards its end. Not for the first time, I was glad to be wrong.

Musicians and artistes are often asked to support charities by giving their services free of charge and over the years I have taken the view that life has been good to me and it is only fair that I give something back. As a result, I have helped many causes by singing a few songs. Sheila tells me that I just cannot say 'no' to a request to do a charity gig and Pat Egan tells me that even at this stage of my life, I have to learn.

Apart from VATS and PATS, I have had a long association with the Variety Club of Ireland, which is headed by Chief Barker Kevin Wall and his wife Betty. The Variety Club has for many years provided buses for clubs and children's organisations and has been the principal outlet through which artistes have made contributions to good causes. The Variety Club of Ireland elected me to its 'Hall of Fame' and I attended a most happy ceremony when I joined an elite group that includes Eamon Andrews, the Irish dancer Rory O'Connor and the legendary Maureen Potter. I have been the recipient of some awards, many of which were linked to fundraising events. I was very honoured however to be nominated as 'Dublin Man of the Year' by the New York Dublin Association and to receive an award before a huge attendance at the famous Terrace on the Park. I was also honoured to receive the Lord Mayor of Dublin award from Cllr. Catherine Byrne at the Mansion House in 2006. Ashford Castle presented me with an award when I sang there for a week in 2000 but my most memorable award presentation was when I was voted a winner in the National Entertainment Awards and was up there alongside Gay Byrne and The Corrs.

Another outstanding occasion was when our President Mary McAleese invited a group of entertainers from the showband era to a reception at Áras an Úachtaráin. We all gathered in the reception room and were introduced individually to the President by broadcaster Jimmy Magee. When it came to my turn, Jimmy did not get a chance to say who I was because President McAleese got in first with 'Oh – it's you, Sonny. You are most welcome. You know I used to dance to your music in Rostrevor when I was growing up.'

It was a moment to treasure.

Pat Egan has been true to his promise to 'look after me'. He has booked me into some high-quality venues such as the Cork Opera House, the Civic Theatre Tallaght, the Helix and the National Concert Hall and we have performed to full houses at all of these venues. He has allowed me to surround myself with some truly professional musicians such as Ray Clifford on keyboards, his wife Linda on drums and guitarist Benny Kindillon who flies over from his home in Spain for gigs. To my great delight, I have also been able to include my great friends Earl Gill on trumpet and Jim Farley on sax in the band.

Getting back up on stage and entertaining people again has been a lifesaver. I could easily have sat at home for the rest of my life getting more grumpy every day and having nothing much to do with myself. Thanks to Sil and Roland, I made it to the National Concert Hall that evening and met with Pat Egan. Today I have a life that is a perfect balance between doing what I love – singing for an audience and being with Sheila. Pat arranges a concert every few weeks and I get to perform at splendid venues with excellent facilities before audiences who know my music and with whom I have struck up a rapport over the years. I think that I am also being introduced to a new audience because many of my loyal supporters are bringing their children, and even grandchildren, to the concerts. When I do these venues, I ask the producers to keep the house lights on so that I can see the audience and communicate with them. This is what I have always done in dance halls, pubs and clubs and it works well for me.

The music that I now perform is principally the songs I have been singing all my life. They are the ballads of Matt Munro, Max Bygraves, Perry Como and Kris Kristofferson. I have rarely strayed outside of this repertoire, which is based on good melodies and romantic lyrics. By doing this, I suppose many styles of music have passed me by. I have never attempted to sing songs by U2, Oasis, Blur or other big groups who have, of course, written tunes with nice melodies and good lyrics but very often the words seem to me to be abstract and just do not rhyme. On one occasion a producer asked me to do something 'outside the box' and suggested a Beatles number. I tried hard to master it – but failed and it did not go into the show. I like to listen to music but again my preference is for the sounds of my youth – the big bands, Frank Sinatra and Bing Crosby and more recent singers in a similar vein such as Harry Connick Junior. Of late I have been attracted to Michael Bublé who is a very fine singer in that genre. Among Irish artistes, my favourites continue to be the showband singers like Dickie Rock, Brendan Bowyer, Tony Kenny and the late Joe Dolan. Among the current generation, I believe that Jack L has a fine voice, a feeling for lyrics, good presentation and is a very talented performer.

I have mixed views about the direction that popular music has taken over the years. It has become louder, more brash and aggressive and seems to lack melody and good lyrics, which are the foundations of a good song. Maybe that is why the Great American Songbook remains as popular today as it was 50 years ago – because it is based on songs which have great tunes and great words. I also think that there is a tendency to dumb down music and popular entertainment – particularly on television. I thoroughly dislike so-called reality television in which ordinary people are subjected to embarrassment and humiliation for the entertainment of viewers. This is particularly true in the case of shows like *The X Factor*, where talented entertainers are subjected to severe criticism, condescension and sarcasm after they have performed to the very best of their ability. Auditions are, of course, a necessary part of selecting artistes or performers for a show but they should be conducted in private with proper respect for the candidates – not on television, before a panel of people who often appear to be more concerned about their own image, rather than the feelings of the entertainers whom they criticise in front of an audience of millions of viewers. The best and only effective way of combating this exploitation of performers is to refuse to watch programmes like that.

In the context of the early death of my father and my two encounters with cancer, it might seem strange to say that I have enjoyed a charmed life. Yet I believe this is the case. In Sheila, I have a real treasure of a wife and a life partner. We have been exceptionally close over the decades and I am as much in love with her now as I was when we first met. We have been blessed with a warm-hearted and loving family who have given us grandchildren and a reason to spend some quality time in Australia, a place which Sheila and I enjoy very much. It is informal, laid back, yet efficient with a 'can do' philosophy of life. The weather is usually good, the standard of living is high and most importantly, the quality of life enjoyed by most of the population is also high by European standards. Geraldine, Gary and Aisling, as well as their partners and children, enjoy life there and we are privileged to share it with them when we visit.

When we are in Ireland, which is most of the time, we lead a contented 'ordinary' life, just as we have done since I stopped travelling with the showbands. We enjoy a trip to Bray for a walk along the prom, meals out with friends, social occasions, the gigs where I sing and which Sheila often attends and our holiday home in Kilmuckridge, which we have refurbished and opened up once again. I would not say that I am over-religious but Sheila and I are both practicing Catholics and during my illness I derived comfort and support from my faith and from Sheila's prayers and those of literally thousands of people from all over the country. Indeed we still get letters from people telling us that they have arranged for Masses and prayers to be said for us – and that is very touching indeed.

The life of an entertainer can, of course, be difficult. The music industry has a reputation for being tough and uncompromising but maybe because I always managed my own affairs, I have never really experienced the bad side of the business. On the contrary, I have enjoyed the good side – the semi-celebrity status, the fact that I am known and recognised almost everywhere I go, the functions and events to which Sheila and I are invited, the appearances on radio and television and even simply seeing my name up there on a poster. All of that is there to be appreciated and enjoyed but it comes with a major health warning – that you should never believe your own publicity. I never really achieved stardom status but I did enjoy respect and recognition as a successful entertainer. Sheila and I never got caught up in the celebrity circuit but instead we have enjoyed the company of a small group who have been friends for most of our lives. We live comfortably in the home we bought before we got married, having done some extensions and additions over the years to make it more comfortable. We are close to our friends and in a neighbourhood that we know and love. Could anything be better?

I am proud of my origins as a Liberties Boy and of being a Dubliner – a citizen of one of the finest cities of the world, steeped as it is, in history, literature and song. I am happy too with what I have achieved in my career. When I first attended Molly Coulihan's stage school or learned to play the sax at the Dublin School of Music, little did I think that I would still be entertaining audiences six decades later.

Yet that is what I do today and hope to do as long as I have the health and strength to keep going.

To keep on singing, to keep on 'washing windows', to keep on smiling and to keep on taking care of your cares with music. *For the Good Times.*

The Author

This book is the result of many
conversations over many
months between Sonny Knowles and
author
and journalist Frank Corr. A native
of Limerick, Frank has worked in
many aspects of journalism and
communications. His books include
Hotels in Ireland, *A Star Reborn* and
Parknasilla.

Previous Publications by Hillgate Publishing Ltd.

Martin Molony – A Legend in his Lifetime
Author: Guy St. John Williams
ISBN 0-95418190-0-5

T. P. Burns – A Racing Life
Author: Guy St. John Williams
ISBN 0-9541819-1-3

The Cheltenham Gold Cup Immortals
Author: Guy St. John Williams
(Limited Edition)

Cecilia Come Back
Gee Gee Al Fan Lie
Author: Sr. Mary Cecilia Delany
Limited edition

Martin Molony – A Legend in his Lifetime

Author: Guy St. John Williams
ISBN 0-95418190-0-5

T. P. Burns – A Racing Life

Author: Guy St. John Williams
ISBN 0-9541819-1-3

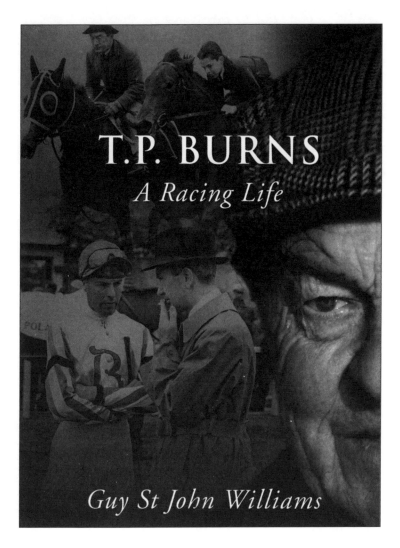